When I Was Your Age

Your Age

VOLUME ONE

When I Was Your Age

VOLUME ONE

Original Stories About Growing Up

Edited and with an introduction
by Amy Ehrlich

CANDLEWICK PRESS
CAMBRIDGE, MASSACHUSETTS

Introduction copyright © 1996 by Amy Ehrlich
"All-Ball" copyright © 1996 by Mary Pope Osborne
"The Great Rat Hunt" copyright © 1996 by Laurence Yep
"Everything Will Be Okay" copyright © 1996 by James Howe
"Why I Never Ran Away From Home" copyright © 1996 by Katherine Paterson
"Reverend Abbott and Those Bloodshot Eyes" copyright © 1996 by Walter Dean Myers
"Muffin" copyright © 1996 by Susan Cooper
"Taking a Dare" copyright © 1996 by Nicholasa Mohr
"Flying" copyright © 1996 by Reeve Lindbergh
"Scout's Honor" copyright © 1996 by Avi
"Blue" copyright © 1996 by Francesca Lia Block

First paperback edition 2001

The Library of Congress has cataloged the hardcover edition as follows:

When I was your age : original stories about growing up / edited with an introduction
by Amy Ehrlich.—1st ed.
Contents: All-ball / by Mary Pope Osborne—The great rat hunt / by Laurence Yep—
Everything will be okay / by James Howe—Why I never ran away from home / by
Katherine Paterson—Reverend Abbott and those bloodshot eyes / by Walter Dean
Myers—Muffin / by Susan Cooper—Taking a dare / by Nicholasa Mohr—Flying / by
Reeve Lindbergh—Scout's honor / by Avi—Blue / by Francesca Lia Block.
ISBN 1-56402-306-0 (hardcover).—ISBN 0-7636-1034-8 (paperback)
1. Authors, American—20th century—Childhood and youth—Juvenile literature.
2. United States—Social life and customs—20th century—Juvenile literature.
3. Children—United States—Biography—Juvenile literature. [1. Authors, American—
Childhood and youth.] I. Ehrlich, Amy, date.
PS129.W44   1996
810.9—dc20   [B]   95-4820

10 9 8 7 6

Printed in the United States of America

This book was typeset in Fairfield and Diotima.
Book design by Virginia Evans

Candlewick Press
2067 Massachusetts Avenue
Cambridge, Massachusetts 02140

CONTENTS

INTRODUCTION

"Tell me a story of when you were a little boy," I used to ask my father, when I was a little girl. Because he happened to be a writer, the stories he told were more romantic than fairy tales, more exciting than TV adventure dramas. Maybe they were even true!

That's what we did when we put together this collection: We sent letters to all ten of the writers, asking them for stories. "If you are interested in this project (we said) the story you might choose to tell doesn't have to be literally true in every detail but should be located in time and space in your own childhood. It can be dramatic or serious or funny—whatever tone is right for the characters and plot."

Each story that came back amazed us. Each was completely different from the others and yet they had so much in common. Perhaps this is because all these writers (and the rest of us too) share childhood itself—a rich and important time in a human life.

Time moves more slowly in childhood. That's probably hard to realize when you are living through it, but think for example how long a summer seems between one school year and the next. The quality of what you see and feel is more vivid too in childhood. When you are very happy or very sad, those emotions color everything. Some of the experiences you are having, even right now, may remain with you always as memories.

Several of the stories in this collection take place more than half a century ago. Television had not yet been invented, and radios and phonographs were the only entertainment in people's homes. There was no MTV, no video arcades, no malls. World War II was going on, yet children played without fear on city streets. Life was very different, but through the lens of the storyteller, you can see what it felt like to be a child in this vanished world.

Walter Dean Myers's "Reverend Abbott and Those Bloodshot Eyes" will take you to Harlem in New York in the late 1940s, when every mother on the block would keep an eye on all the children and holler if anyone misbehaved. And with the boys in Avi's story "Scout's Honor," you can take the subway all the way from Brooklyn to Manhattan and walk across the George Washington Bridge, afraid not of muggers but only of dishonoring yourself in front of your friends.

For all the writers in this collection, the places they describe so vividly are the places where they grew up. These are special places yet ordinary; taken for granted at the time but etched and glowing in memory. Quite simply, they are home.

Listen to Mary Pope Osborne in her story "All-Ball" describe the army posts of the 1950s: "I loved the neat lawns, clean streets, trim houses, and starched uniforms. I loved parade bands, marching troops, green jeeps, tanks, and transport trucks.... Living on an army post in those days was so safe that in all the early summers of our lives the children of our family were let out each morning like dandelions to the wind."

Just as home is the place known best, so are children's families the center of the world in these stories. In fact, more than half of them are about a child's intense love for another family member—mother, father, sister, brother. Most often, this beloved person understands the child's longings and responds in a full and loving way.

Beneath the humor of Laurence Yep's "The Great Rat Hunt" is the poignant story of a boy's relationship with his father. The child narrator, who has asthma, cannot impress his father with his athletic ability; and yet his father lets the boy know that he is loved for who he is. What could be a more important gift from a parent to a child?

In Reeve Lindbergh's "Flying," another kind of understanding is involved. When her aviator father tries to teach his children about airplanes by taking them up in a small plane on Saturday afternoons, the lesson instead is about what flying means to *him*.

Brothers and sisters too—particularly older ones—can be a powerful influence on children. In Katherine Paterson's "Why I Never Ran Away from Home," set in wartime China, it is her bullying big sister Lizzie—

prettier and more talented (or so the narrator thinks)—who stops her from doing something disastrous.

But a family's love can also be destructive. In some of the stories, children are very needy and vulnerable, and the writers show that if parents or brothers or sisters ignore this, the child can be badly hurt.

In Francesca Lia Block's "Blue," a girl's father, sad and distant since his wife deserted them, does not see his daughter's despair until it is almost too late. And in James Howe's "Everything Will Be Okay," a boy's longing for a stray kitten collides hard with his brother's code about toughness.

In fact, the need to be tough is a strong undercurrent to many of the stories in this collection. Despite environments that are often safe and welcoming, the cruelty of other people—particularly people their own age—exposes children to danger and sometimes makes toughness the only possible response.

Taunts like "Crybaby," "Stupid," "Wacko," and "Sissy"; and phrases like "I felt lonely," "I was scared," "I couldn't stop crying" come up in these stories repeatedly. Childhood can be a harsh and friendless time.

In Susan Cooper's wartime story "Muffin," a schoolyard bully called Fat Alice scares Daisy, the heroine, far more than the bombs falling in England during the Blitz. Fat Alice is truly evil; her meanness has no apparent motive or cause. She kicks, trips, shoves, and pinches while the adults are busy elsewhere.

What is a child to do against such terrorism? Resourcefulness is certainly required. But so too is real certainty and self-confidence. Throughout this collection, the question of identity—what it is and how you get it—comes up over and over again.

In the stories, children define themselves by their similarities and differences to their siblings and parents. In Nicholasa Mohr's "Taking a Dare," for example, it takes real nerve for the narrator to find her own path between her mother's intense and unquestioning Catholicism and the atheism of her socialist father.

But there are times when children, for their survival, must move away from their families and carve out new identities all their own, and this is a process that does not seem to come easily.

In fact, most of the stories in *When I Was Your Age* have some emotional pain in them. Their child heroes are self-conscious or ill at ease in the world. Some suffer at unfair circumstances (such as the death or disappearance of a parent), while others are just simply filled with pain—crying and miserable and alone. *Different.*

What is the answer? What can children do aside from learning to be tough, which is only a temporary or at best a partial answer? I believe that an uncanny number of the stories in this collection show another more creative path—the transformation of suffering through art.

Clues to it are everywhere in the stories. But perhaps the clearest comes from Francesca Lia Block's "Blue." In the end, it is only when the heroine, La, writes about her vanished mother that her terrible pain stops. The words she writes also have the effect of connecting other people to her:

> "Daddy," La said.
> When she handed him the story, his eyes changed.
> "It's about Mom," La said, but she knew he knew....
> "Thank you, honey." He looked as though he hadn't slept or eaten for days. But he took off his glasses then, and La saw two small images of herself swimming in the tears in his eyes.

*   *   *

Where does writing begin? What is it that shapes writers? If we want to look for the seeds of it in childhood, I think this collection makes it clear that they have probably been there for a very long time.

Isolation and separation can be bridged by language. Words can cross time and distance, connecting people of different generations and ages and experience. As you read the stories in *When I Was Your Age,* think of the grown-up writers who were once children. Here they are; this is what they saw and felt and remembered.

Listen carefully. They are telling you their stories.

—AMY EHRLICH

Mary Pope Osborne

ALL-BALL

~

MARY   POPE   OSBORNE

I remember the first time I got really bad news.

I was eight years old, and my family was living in white wooden army quarters at the edge of a thick pine forest in Fort Eustis, Virginia. All my life we had lived on military posts, and I loved them. I loved the neat lawns, clean streets, trim houses, and starched uniforms. I loved parade bands, marching troops, green jeeps, tanks, and transport trucks. I loved having military police at the entrance gate. When I was four, I dreamed that the M.P.'s guarding the gate chased away a couple of ghosts that tried to come onto our post. It is one of the most vivid dreams I've ever had, and to this day, it makes me feel good to remember it.

Living on an army post in those days was so safe that in all the early summers of our lives the children of our family were let out each morning like dandelions to the wind. My teenage sister went off with her friends while my brothers and I filled our time playing with our toy soldiers, including my favorite—a small silver statue of General Omar Bradley. We played "maneuvers" by carrying large cardboard boxes around the parade field, stopping every hundred yards to "bivouac" by making grass beds and napping inside our boxes.

At five o'clock, when the bugle played and the flag was lowered, we went home. Our return was often punctuated by the joyous sight of our dad stepping out of a chauffeured military car, his arms raised to embrace us.

But one spring night when I was eight, bad news changed everything. I remember my dad was helping me prepare my bath. I was sitting on the edge of the tub while the water ran, and Dad was standing in the doorway, wearing his summer khaki uniform. "Sis—" he always called me Sis or Little Bits—"in six weeks, Daddy is going to Korea."

I looked at him and burst into tears. I knew we wouldn't be going with him. Though the Korean War had ended eight years earlier, U.S. soldiers were still sent there for tours of duty—without their families.

"Don't cry," he said. "I'll only be gone for a year."

Only a year?

"While I'm gone, you'll live in Florida, in Daytona Beach, near the ocean."

Daytona Beach? Away from an army post?

"You'll have a wonderful time."

"No I won't!" I hated this news. And to prove it, I pushed him out of the bathroom.

Of course, I was right and he was wrong. A few weeks later, when Dad drove our family to Daytona Beach to get us settled, I didn't find our new life wonderful at all.

Our house was low to the ground, flamingo-pink, and made of stucco. There were no kids in the whole neighborhood. There were no real trees in our small yard—just a few scrubby ones. There was no wide open parade field to play on.

I recoiled from this new life—especially when I discovered lizards scampering across our cement driveway, a huge water bug scuttling across the floor of the TV room, and a gigantic black spider hovering in the corner of the garage. Such monsters didn't exist on army posts—neither did the crazy variety of houses, the litter, the tawdry seaside billboards.

Adding to the trauma of adjusting to life off a military post was the awareness that my dad was leaving in just three weeks. At first, I tried to manage my grief by taking a little time out of every day to cry. In those days, I was very organized. I kept a daily list of things to do like:

> *Wash hands*
> *Play with dolls*
> *Practice writing*
> *Practice running*

I added "Cry for Daddy" to the list. But as I counted

down the days till his departure, I began to cry even when it wasn't scheduled. Worse, I abandoned the other things on my list to keep a watch on my dad. I studied everything he did—from buying a vanilla ice-cream cone at the Dairy Queen to playing catch with my brothers—because I felt I had to store up enough memories of him to last through the coming year.

The pressure became unbearable and soon forced me into the strangest relationship of my life. Just thinking about this relationship now can bring tears to my eyes. Was it with a wonderful girl? Boy? Grown-up? Dog, cat, parakeet?

No. It was with a *ball*.

About two weeks before Dad left, he took my brothers and me to a Rose's Five & Dime store. He gave us fifty cents each to buy whatever we wanted.

This is the most precious fifty cents I will ever spend, I thought. Slowly, I wandered the rows of comics, coloring books, plastic dolls, and bags of candy, looking for an object worthy of the last-fifty-cents-my-father-gave-me-before-he-went-to-Korea.

When I came to the ball section, I saw, amidst a variety of balls, a truly unique specimen: a nubby rubber ball, bigger than a softball and smaller than a kickball. It was made up of swirling pastel colors—pink, blue, green.

I picked up the ball and bounced it.

It was the best bouncing ball I'd ever encountered. Barely did it touch the wooden floor before it sprang back into my hands. The ball felt friendly, spunky, and vibrant. It had such a positive and strong personality that I named it before we even got home: All-Ball.

For the next twelve days, All-Ball and I were inseparable. I bounced him on the driveway and on the sidewalk. Standing apart from everyone, deep in my own world, I bounced him for hours. And while I bounced, I talked to myself. I invented stories. Not dramatic stories of high-adventure. But stories about ordinary families—families in which everyone stayed together and everyone was safe and secure.

In these families, there was perfect order. The children all had names that began with the same letter—David, Danny, and Doris; Paul, Peter, and Patsy; Anne, Alice, Adam, and Ace.

I gave the children ages, personalities, and dialogue. I played all the parts. I was John joking with Jane; Jane laughing with Jack; Adam telling a story to Ace; Alice describing her school outfits to Anne.

I lived in different families morning, afternoon, and twilight. I could only create these worlds with All-Ball's help. His sprightly, joyous attitude gave me confidence. The sound of his rhythmic bounce banished my fears. His constant presence eased the sorrow of Dad's leaving. In fact, whenever Dad tried to engage me in conversation or play, I turned away from him. I stopped paying attention to him altogether.

I had fallen in love with a ball.

Though everyone in my family must have thought my behavior odd, they adjusted quickly. Within a day or two, they were treating "Sis's ball" sort of like a family pet.

No one, however, was fully aware of the depth of my attachment until the morning All-Ball was destroyed.

It was a hot, bright July morning—just two days before Dad was to leave for Korea. I was outside before everyone else, bouncing All-Ball on the sidewalk, inventing a family with a neat number of years between each child. I liked the children to be ten, eight, six, four. Boy, girl, boy, girl. John, Jane, Jed, Joy.

While I was bouncing All-Ball in the early warm air, a small black dog wandered down the sidewalk to see what was up, a little dog I paid no attention to—until it was too late. And then everything happened so fast, I couldn't stop it.

I fumbled a bounce. The black dog charged and grabbed All-Ball in his mouth. He punctured the rubber skin with his teeth, then shook the deflated ball with glee, tearing it to pieces. I started to scream. I screamed and screamed.

Everyone rushed out to their yards—old people from all the quiet, lonely houses. My parents, brothers, sister. I couldn't stop screaming as I ran around, picking up all the torn patches of All-Ball. I clutched them to my chest and howled at the top of my lungs.

My mother explained to the neighbors that my ball had popped. My brothers and sister watched me in horror—my father in confusion. "We'll get you another ball," he said.

He couldn't have uttered crueler words. There was no other ball like All-Ball. Not in the whole world. Not with his spirit, his bounce, his steadfastness. I screamed "No!" with such rage that everyone retreated.

I ran inside, and, clutching the pieces of All-Ball, I went to bed, yelling at everyone to leave us alone. I kissed the pastel-colored nubby skin and sobbed and sobbed.

I did not get up all day. I grieved for the death of All-Ball with all the grief my eight years could muster. I was brought lunch, cool drinks, newspaper comics, wet washcloths for my head, children's aspirin. But nothing worked. I would not get up. I would not let go of the torn pieces of the ball.

At twilight, I could hear the family having dinner in the dining room. My mother had the decency to allow me to work out my sorrow on my own. I don't think she even allowed anyone to laugh.

As light faded across my room, I could hear sprinklers spritzing outside, and an old woman calling to her cats. By now, my eyes stung and were nearly swollen shut.

My throat burned. My heart had not stopped hurting all day.

"Little Bits?" My father stood in my doorway. He was holding a ball. It was mostly white with a little bit of blue.

I moaned and turned my face to the wall as he walked toward the bed.

"You won't let me give you this new ball?" he said.

"No!" I said, gasping with another wave of grief. "Go away!"

"This ball's pretty nice," he said.

Closing my eyes, I shook my head emphatically, furious he did not understand the difference between the ball he held and All-Ball. "I hate it! Go away!"

He didn't. He sat on the edge of the bed.

But I would not look at him. My burning eyes stared at the wall. My body was stiff with anger.

"I like your barrette," he said softly.

He was referring to a pink Scottie dog barrette locked onto my tangled hair.

I didn't speak.

He cleared his throat. "I hope you'll wear that the day I come home."

I blinked. The truth was I hadn't thought much about his coming home. Only about his leaving.

"I'll bring you a ring when I come back," he said.

I didn't move. Just blinked again.

"What kind of ring would you like?"

I mumbled something.

"What?" he asked.

"A pearl," I said hoarsely.

"A pearl ring. Okay. On the day I come home, I'll bring you a pearl ring. And a music box. How's that? I'll hide in the bushes, and when you ride up on your bike, home from school, I'll jump out and surprise you. How's that?"

He cleared his throat again. I turned just a little to look at him. I saw he had tears in his eyes. I didn't want him to feel sad too. That was almost worse than anything.

I reluctantly rolled over onto my back. I looked at the ball he held. It was still a stupid ball, no doubt about that. But I mumbled something about it being pretty.

"Will you play with this one?" he said.

I touched it with my finger. I let out a quivering sigh, then nodded, accepting the complications of the moment. All-Ball would know that he could never be replaced. Ever. He was the one and only ball for me. But I could pretend to like this other one. Even play with it. For Dad's sake.

He handed me the white ball and I embraced it and smiled feebly.

He smiled back. "Come eat some dinner with us now," he said.

I was ready. I wanted to leave my room. The light of day was nearly gone.

"Come on." He helped me off the bed, and, clutching pieces of All-Ball along with the new white ball, I joined the family.

My dad left soon after that. We entered a new school. Ball-bouncing was replaced with friends, homework, and writing letters to Korea. Still—and this is weird, I'll admit—I slept with a torn piece of All-Ball under my pillow for the next year, until after my dad came home.

~≈

Notes from
MARY POPE OSBORNE

"I decided to share the story of All-Ball with young readers because I think it speaks to the hardest thing about being a child: the fact that most things in your life are out of your control. On the other hand, it also shows one of the best things about being a child: the fact that you can use your imagination to help ease your troubles.

All the games I once played—from talking to All-Ball, to playing with my dolls, to pretending to be a cowboy or a soldier with my brothers— helped me become a writer. And one of the great joys of being a writer is that every day I can still use my imagination to help ease my troubles. The spirit of All-Ball now lives in my writing tools, instead of in a beloved rubber ball."

Laurence Yep

THE
GREAT RAT HUNT

LAURENCE YEP

I had asthma when I was young, so I never got to play sports much with my father. While my brother and father practiced, I could only sit in bed, propped up by a stack of pillows. As I read my comic books, I heard them beneath our apartment window. In the summer, it was the thump of my brother's fastball into my father's mitt. In the fall, it was the smack of a football. In the winter, it was the airy bounce of a basketball.

Though my father had come from China when he was eight, he had taken quickly to American games. When he and Mother were young, they had had the same dances and sports leagues as their white school-mates—but kept separate in Chinatown. (He had met Mother when she tripped him during a co-ed basketball game at the Chinatown Y).

Father was big as a teenager and good at sports. In

fact, a social club in Chinatown had hired him to play football against social clubs in other Chinatowns. There he was, a boy playing against grown men.

During a game in Watsonville, a part-time butcher had broken Father's nose. It never properly healed, leaving a big bump at the bridge. There were other injuries too from baseball, basketball, and tennis. Each bump and scar on his body had its own story, and each story was matched by a trophy or medal.

Though he now ran a grocery store in San Francisco, he tried to pass on his athletic skills to my older brother Eddy and me. During the times I felt well, I tried to keep up with them, but my lungs always failed me.

When I had to sit down on the curb, I felt as if I had let my father down. I'd glance up anxiously when I felt his shadow over me; but he looked neither angry nor disgusted—just puzzled, as if he could not understand why my lungs were not like his.

"S-s-sorry." I panted.

"That's okay." He squatted and waved his hat, trying to fan more air at me. In the background, Eddy played catch with himself, waiting impatiently for the lessons to begin again. Ashamed, I would gasp. "Go on...and play."

And Father and Eddy would start once more while I watched, doomed to be positively un-American, a weakling, a perpetual spectator, an outsider. Worse, I felt as if Eddy were Father's only true son.

And then came the day when the rat invaded our store. It was Eddy who first noticed it while we were re-stocking the store shelves. I was stacking packages of pinto beans when Eddy called me. "Hey, do you know what this is?" He waved me over to the cans of soup. On his palm lay some dark drops. "Is it candy?"

Father came out of the storeroom in the rear of our store. Over his back, he carried a huge hundred pound sack of rice. He let it thump to the floor right away. "Throw that away."

"What is it, Father?" I asked.

"Rat droppings," he said. "Go wash your hands."

"Yuck." Eddy flung the droppings down.

While Eddy washed his hands, I helped Father get rid of the evidence. Then he got some wooden traps from a shelf and we set them out.

However, the traps were for mice and not for rats. The rat must have gotten a good laugh while it stole the bait and set off the springs.

Then Father tried poison pellets, but the rat avoided them all. It even left a souvenir right near the front door.

Father looked grim as he cleaned it up. "I'm through fooling around."

So he called up his exterminator friend, Pete Wong, the Cockroach King of Chinatown. While Pete fumigated the store, we stayed with my Aunt Nancy over on Mason, where the cable cars kept me up late. They always rang their bells when they rounded the corner. Even when they weren't there, I could hear the cable rattling in its channel beneath the street. It was OK, though, because my cousin Jackie could tell stories all night.

The next day, when we went back home, Father searched around the store, sniffing suspiciously for deadly chemicals. Mother went upstairs to our apartment over the store to get our electric fan.

She came right back down empty-handed. "I think he's moved up there. I could hear him scratching behind the living room walls."

Father stared at the ceiling as if the rat had gone too far. "Leave it to me," he said. He fished his car keys from his pocket.

"Where are you going?" Mother asked.

Father, though, was a man of few words. He preferred to speak by his actions. "I'll be back soon."

An hour and a half later he returned with a rifle. He held it up for the three of us to examine. "Isn't it a beaut? Henry Loo loaned it to me." Henry Loo was a pharmacist and one of Father's fishing buddies.

Mother frowned. "You can't shoot that cannon off in my house."

"It's just a twenty-two." Father tugged a box of cartridges out of his jacket pocket. "Let's go, boys."

Mother sucked in her breath sharply. "Thomas!"

Father was surprised by Mother's objection. "They've got to learn sometime."

Mother turned to us urgently. "It means killing. Like buying Grandpop's chickens. But you'll be the ones who have to make it dead."

"It's not the same," Father argued. "We won't have to twist its neck."

Buying the chicken was a chore that everyone tried to avoid at New Year's when Mother's father insisted on it. To make sure the chicken was fresh, we had to watch the poulterer kill it. And then we had to collect the coppery-smelling blood in a jar for a special dish that only Mother's father would eat. For a moment, I felt queasy.

"You're scaring the boys," Father scolded her.

Mother glanced at him over her shoulder. "They ought to know what they're getting into."

I didn't believe in killing—unless it was a bug like a cockroach. However, I felt different when I saw a real rifle—the shiny barrel, the faint smell of oil, the decorated wooden stock. I rationalized the hunt by telling myself I was not murdering rabbits or deer, just a mean old rat—like a furry kind of cockroach.

"What'll it be, boys?" Father asked.

Taking a deep breath, I nodded my head. "Yes, sir."

Father turned expectantly to Eddy and raised an eyebrow.

From next to me, though, Eddy murmured, "I think I'll help Mother." He wouldn't look at me.

Father seemed just as shocked as Mother and I. "Are you sure?"

Eddy drew back and mumbled miserably. "Yes, sir."

Mother gave me a quick peck on the cheek. "I expect you to still have ten toes and ten fingers when you finish."

As we left the store, I felt funny. Part of me felt triumphant. For once, it was Eddy who had failed and not me. And yet another part of me wished I were staying with him and Mother.

Father said nothing as we left the store and climbed the back stairs. As I trailed him, I thought he was silent because he was disappointed: He would rather have Eddy's help than mine.

At the back door of our apartment, he paused and said brusquely, "Now for some rules. First, never, never aim the rifle at anyone."

I listened as attentively as I had the disastrous times he'd tried to teach me how to dribble, or catch a football, or handle a pop foul. "I won't." I nodded earnestly.

Father pulled a lever near the middle of the gun. "Next, make sure the rifle is empty." He let me inspect the breech. There was nothing inside.

"Yes, sir," I said and glanced up at him to read his mood. Because Father used so few words, he always sounded a little impatient whenever he taught me a lesson. However, it was hard to tell this time if it was genuine irritation or his normal reserve.

He merely grunted. "Here. Open this." And he handed me the box of cartridges.

I was so nervous that the cartridges clinked inside the box when I took it. As I fumbled at the lid, I almost felt like apologizing for not being Eddy.

Now, when I got edgy, I was the opposite of Father: I got talkier. "How did you learn how to hunt?" I asked. "From your father?"

My father rarely spoke of his father, who had died before I was born. He winced now as if the rat had just nipped him. "My old man? Nah. He never had the time. I learned from some of my buddies in Chinatown." He held out his hand.

I passed him a cartridge. "What did you hunt? Bear?"

"We shot quail." Father carefully loaded the rifle.

I was uncomfortable with the idea of shooting the cute little birds I saw in cartoons. "You did?"

He clicked the cartridge into the rifle. "You have to be tough in this world, boy. There are going to be some times when nobody's around to help—like when I first came to America."

That was a long speech for Father. "You had your father." His mother had stayed back in China, because in those days, America would not let her accompany her husband.

"He was too busy working." Father stared back down the stairs as if each step were a year. "When I first came here, I got beaten up by the white kids. And when the white kids weren't around, there were the other Chinese kids."

I furrowed my forehead in puzzlement. I handed him another cartridge. "But they were your own kind."

He loaded the rifle steadily as I gave him the ammunition. "No, they weren't. The boys born here, they like to give a China-born a hard time. They thought I'd be easy pickings. But it was always a clean fight. No knives. No guns. Just our feet and fists. Not like the punks nowadays." He snapped the last cartridge into the rifle. "Then I learned how to play their games, and I made them my friends." He said the last part with pride.

And suddenly I began to understand all the trophies and medals in our living room. They were more than awards for sports. Each prize was a sign that my father belonged to America—and at the same time, to Chinatown. And that was why he tried so hard now to teach sports to Eddy and me.

When I finally understood what sports really meant to my father, it only magnified the scale of my ineptitude. "I'm not good at fighting." As I closed the lid on the box of ammunition, I thought I ought to prepare him for future disappointments. "I'm not much good at anything."

Careful to keep the rifle pointed away from me, Father unlocked the door. "I said you have to be tough, not stupid. No reason to get a beat-up old mug like mine."

I shook my head, bewildered. "What's wrong with your face?"

Father seemed amused. He stepped away from the door and jerked his head for me to open it. "It's nothing that a steamroller couldn't fix."

"But you have an interesting face," I protested as I grabbed the doorknob.

"Are you blind, boy? This mug isn't ever going to win a beauty contest." He chuckled. "I've been called a lot of names in my time, but never 'interesting.' You've got a way with words."

The doorknob was cold in my hand. "I do?"

Father adjusted his grip on the rifle. "I wouldn't buy any real estate from you." And he gave me an encouraging grin. "Now let's kill that rat."

When I opened the door, our home suddenly seemed as foreign to me as Africa. At first, I felt lonely—and a little scared. Then I heard Father reassure me, "I'm with you, boy."

Feeling more confident, I crept through the kitchen and into the living room. Father was right behind me and motioned me to search one half of the room while he explored the other. When I found a hole in the corner away from the fireplace, I caught Father's eye and pointed.

He peered under a chair with me and gave me an approving wink. "Give me a hand," he whispered.

In silent cooperation, we moved the chair aside and then shifted the sofa over until it was between us and the rat hole. Bit by bit, Father and I constructed an up-holstered barricade. I couldn't have been prouder if we'd built a whole fort together.

Father considerately left the lighter things for me to lift, and I was grateful for his thoughtfulness. The last thing I wanted was to get asthma now from overexertion. When we were done, Father got his rifle from the corner where he had left it temporarily.

As we crouched down behind our improvised wall, Father rested the rifle on it. "We'll take turns watching."

"Yes, sir," I said, peering over the barrier. There wasn't so much as a whisker in the hole.

While I scanned the hole with intense radar eyes, Father tried to make himself comfortable by leaning against the sofa. It made me feel important to know Father trusted me; and I was determined to do well. In the center of the living room wall was the fireplace, and on its mantel stood Father's trophies like ranks of soldiers reminding me to be vigilant.

We remained in companionable silence for maybe three quarters of an hour. Suddenly, I saw something flicker near the mouth of the hole. "Father," I whispered.

Father popped up alertly and took his rifle. Squeezing one eye shut, he sighted on the rat hole. His crouching body grew tense. "Right." He adjusted his aim minutely. "Right. Take a breath," he recited to himself. "Take up the slack. Squeeze the trigger." Suddenly, he looked up, startled. "Where'd it go?"

As the gray shape darted forward, I could not control my panic. "It's coming straight at us."

The rifle barrel swung back and forth wildly as Father tried to aim. "Where?"

I thought I could see huge teeth and beady, violent eyes. The teeth were the size of daggers and the eyes were the size of baseballs, and they were getting bigger by the moment. It was the rat of all rats. "Shoot it!" I yelled.

"Where?" Father shouted desperately.

My courage evaporated. All I could think of was escape. "It's charging." Springing to my feet, I darted from the room.

"Oh, man," Father said, and his footsteps pounded after me.

In a blind panic, I bolted out of the apartment and down the back stairs and into the store.

"Get the SPCA. I think the rat's mad," Father yelled as he slammed the door behind him.

Mother took the rifle from him. "I'd be annoyed too if someone were trying to shoot me."

"No." Father panted. "I mean it's rabid." We could hear the rat scurrying above us in the living room. It sounded as if it were doing a victory dance.

Mother made Father empty the rifle. "You return that to Henry Loo tomorrow," she said. "We'll learn to live with the rat."

As she stowed the rifle in the storeroom, Father tried to regather his dignity. "It may have fleas," he called after her.

Now that my panic was over, I suddenly became aware of the enormity of what I had done. Father had counted on me to help him, and yet I had run, leaving him to the ravages of that monster. I was worse than a failure. I was a coward. I had deserted Father right at the time he needed me most. I wouldn't blame him if he kicked me out of his family.

It took what little nerve I had left to look up at my father. At that moment, he seemed to tower over me, as grand and remote as a monument. "I'm sorry," I said miserably.

He drew his eyebrows together as he clinked the shells in his fist. "For what?"

It made me feel even worse to have to explain in front of Eddy. "For running," I said wretchedly.

He chuckled as he dumped the cartridges into his shirt pocket. "Well, I ran too. Sometimes it's smart to be scared."

"When were you ever scared?" I challenged him.

He buttoned his pocket. "Plenty of times. Like when I came to America. They had to pry my fingers from the boat railing."

It was the first time I'd ever heard my father confess to that failing. "But you're the best at everything."

"Nobody's good at everything." He gave his head a little shake as if the very notion puzzled him. "Each of us is good at some things and lousy at others. The trick is to find something that you're good at."

I thought again of the mantel where all of Father's sports trophies stood. Eddy gave every promise of collecting just as many, but I knew I would be lucky to win even one.

"I'm lousy at sports," I confessed.

His eyes flicked back and forth, as if my face were a book open for his inspection. He seemed surprised by what he read there.

Slowly his knees bent until we were looking eye to eye. "Then you'll find something else," he said and put his arm around me. My father never let people touch him. In fact, I hardly ever saw him hug Mother. As his arm tightened, I felt a real love and assurance in that embrace.

Shortly after that, the rat left as mysteriously as it had come. "I must've scared it off," Father announced.

Mother shook her head. "That rat laughed itself to death."

Father disappeared into the storeroom; and for a moment we all thought Mother had gone too far. Then we heard the electric saw that he kept back there. "What are you doing?" Mother called.

He came back out with a block of wood about two inches square. He was carefully sandpapering the splinters from the edges. "Maybe some day we'll find the corpse. Its head ought to look real good over the fireplace."

Mother was trying hard to keep a straight face. "You can't have a trophy head unless you shoot it."

"If it died of laughter like you said, then I killed it," he insisted proudly. "Sure as if I pulled the trigger." He winked at me. "Get the varnish out for our trophy will you?"

I was walking away when I realized he had said "our." I turned and said, "That rat was doomed from the start." I heard my parents both laughing as I hurried away.

"I had no intention to be a writer, but a chemist as my father had wanted to be. However, under the prodding of a high school English teacher, the Reverend John Becker, I began submitting stories to magazines. Much to my surprise, I sold my first story to a science fiction magazine when I was eighteen.

I had all the material I needed for future stories in my family, neighbors, and friends. The story I've told here is a much-cherished family story. Though my father was born in China, he came over here as a boy and learned all sorts of American sports. In fact, before we had the store, he was a playground director and basketball coach in San Francisco's Chinatown.

Unlike my athletic older brother, I never mastered the vagaries of dribbling a basketball or catching a pop fly, despite years of practice. Even so, my father did his best to hide his disappointment. Later, he took great pride in my books; and, in lieu of athletic trophies, he displayed the various plaques, bowls, and medals that I received for my stories."

EVERYTHING WILL BE OKAY

JAMES HOWE

The kitten is a scrawny thing with burrs and bits of wood caught in its hair, where it still has hair, and pus coming out its eyes and nose. Its big baby head looks even bigger at the end of such a stick of a body. I found it in the woods at the end of my street where I play most days with my friends. This time I was alone. Lucky for you I was, I think to the kitten. Otherwise, David or Claude might have decided you'd be good practice for their slingshots. Those two can be mean, I think to myself. I don't like playing with them really, but they live at the end of the street and sometimes you just play with the kids on your same street, even if they're mean, sometimes even to you.

The kitten makes a pitiful noise.

"Don't worry," I tell it, stroking its scabby head until the mewing is replaced by a faint purr. "Everything will be okay. I'm going to take you home, and my mom will give you a bath and some medicine."

I tuck the kitten under my jacket and run out of the

woods, across the street, down the sidewalk toward my house. I feel the warmth of the kitten through my shirt and start thinking of names.

I'm only ten, so it will be five or six years before I work for Dr. Milk. My two oldest brothers worked for him part-time and summers when they were teenagers. Now my other brother, Paul, works there. Dr. Milk is the vet out on Ridge Road. He takes care of our dogs, and he will take care of my kitten.

I never had a pet that was my very own. A couple of years ago, my father got a new beagle to replace the old one who had died, Patches was his name. He called the new one Bucky and said that Bucky could be mine. But saying a thing is so doesn't mean it is.

Bucky lives in a kennel out back, keeping his beagle smell, which my mother hates, far away from the house. I feed Bucky some days and play with him, but I am not allowed to bring him inside to sleep at the end of my bed or curl up next to me while I do my homework. Bucky is an outdoor dog; he is a hunting dog.

He is my father's dog, really.

When I am older, I will go hunting with my father the way my brothers have done. I try not to think about this. I want to go, because I want my father to like me. But I don't want to kill animals.

One time when my father and three brothers went hunting, one of my brothers killed a deer. Most times they kill rabbits or pheasants if they get lucky. Most times they don't get lucky. But this time one of my brothers, I don't remember which one, killed a deer.

The deer was hung by its feet from a tree just outside the kitchen. I could see it hanging there when I sat at my place at the table. My father urged me to eat my venison and talked about the slippers he was going to have made from the hide. I couldn't eat. The thought of the venison made me want to throw up.

I could see the deer's eyes, even from the kitchen table. There was life in them, still. Only the deer and I knew that there was life the bullet had missed. It was in the eyes.

I pushed the venison away.

My father said, "That's a waste of good meat."

My brothers teased me. One of them called me a sissy.

My mother said, "You don't have to eat it," and took the slab of gray meat off my plate.

My mother reaches into my jacket and removes the kitten by the scruff of its neck. She tells me to go down to the cellar and take off all my clothes and put them in a pile next to the washing machine.

"This animal is filled with disease," she says. "We can't let it touch anything in the house."

"We'll take it to Dr. Milk," I say. "He'll make it better."

"We'll see," she says, pushing me toward the cellar stairs, the kitten dangling from one of her hands.

I can feel tears welling up. "But that kitten is *mine*," I say. "I found it and it's going to be my pet."

She doesn't say anything. Looking up from the cellar stairs, I see her shaking her head at the kitten. Its eyes are clamped shut. I can see the pus oozing out of them.

"You are a sorry sight," she tells the kitten in the same soothing voice she uses with me when I'm sick. "A sorry sad sight."

I feel in the pit of my stomach what the future of that kitten is. The feeling spreads through me like a sudden fever. Down in the cellar taking off my clothes, I cry so hard my body shakes.

When I return upstairs, my mother wraps me in my bathrobe and holds me until I can speak.

"Where's the kitten?" I ask.

"Out on the back porch in a box. Your brother will be home soon."

Paul will be going to college in the fall. Right now he's a senior in high school. I can't decide if I'm going to miss him or not. He's the brother I know best because he's been around the longest. The others left home when I was even younger.

Paul is the brother who taught me to ride my bicycle and the one who spent an entire Saturday with me and not his friends building a real igloo out of snow and ice. He's the brother who tells me how to be a man.

He is also the brother who plays tricks on me and sometimes the tricks are cruel. When I get angry, he says I don't have a sense of humor. He twists my arm behind my back sometimes until I say I'll do what he wants me to do. He makes promises he doesn't keep.

Paul is seventeen. He shaves every day and kisses girls right in front of me like it was nothing. He works at Dr. Milk's part-time and summers.

I am sitting on the back porch waiting for Paul to come home and talking to the box next to me.

"Don't worry, Smoky," I tell the kitten inside. "I won't let anything bad happen to you, I don't care how sick you are. My big brother will take you to Dr. Milk's and give you shots and medicine and stuff and you'll get better, you'll see. My big brother can fix anything."

The kitten is awfully quiet. I wish it would make even a pitiful noise.

We sit in silence. I daydream that I am seventeen. I am big and strong like my brother and I can make Smoky better. I see myself driving to Dr. Milk's out on Ridge Road, carrying the kitten in its box into the back room (which I have never seen, really, only heard my brothers tell stories about), giving it some medicine, reassuring it . . .

"Everything will be okay, Smoky, everything will be okay."

In the kitchen behind me I hear my brother and mother talking in low voices.

Dr. Milk is not there when my brother pulls the car into the parking lot. It is after hours. My brother has a key. I am impressed by this.

"Come on," Paul says in his take-charge voice, "get that box now. Bring it on in here."

He flicks on the light in the waiting room. "You're coming in back with me," he commands. "I'll need your help."

"What are you going to do?" I ask. I am holding the box tight against my chest. I feel Smoky moving around inside.

"What do you think?" he says. "You heard your mother. That kitten is sick, bad sick."

"She's your mother, too."

"Well, she happens to be right," Paul tells me. "With an animal that far gone, you don't have a choice. It's got to be put to sleep."

I think the tears I jam back into my body are going to kill me. I think if I don't let them out they will kill me. But I won't let them out. I won't let Paul see.

"You *do* have a choice" is all I say. I hug the box for dear life and move to the door. Paul moves faster.

"Come on now," he says, gently taking hold of my arm, "be a man."

"I'm not a man," I tell him. "I don't want to be."

"You've got to do what's right. That kitten is half dead as it is."

"Then it's half alive, too."

He shakes his head. "You always have to one-up me, don't you?" he says.

I don't know what he means, but I do know that no matter what I say he is going to do what he wants to do.

A few minutes later, we are in the back room. The box is empty. Smoky is inside a big old pretzel can with a hose attached, clawing at the can's sides as my brother pumps in the gas. He is telling me it is good for me to watch this, it will toughen me up, help me be more of a man. Then he starts to lecture me about different methods of putting animals out of their misery, but all I can hear is the scratching. And then the silence.

At the supper table that night, I don't speak. I don't look at my brother's face or my father's or my mother's. I look at the tree branch outside the kitchen window where the deer once hung. My brother is saying something about taking me to the driving range tomorrow. He will teach me to hit a golf ball.

I won't go with him. I don't want him teaching me anything anymore.

In the fall he will go off to college. I will be eleven. I will be alone with my parents, alone without my brothers.

I get up from the table and no one stops me.

In the living room which is dark I sit for a long time thinking. I think about my kitten. I think about the pretzel can. I think about what it will be like not having any brothers around. I feel alone and small and frightened. And then all of a sudden I don't feel any of those things. All of a sudden it's as if Paul has already left and I am on my own and I know some things so clearly that I will never have to ask an older brother to help me figure them out.

I will never work for Dr. Milk.

I will not go hunting with my father.

I will decide for myself what kind of boy I am, what kind of man I will become.

❧

"When I was asked to write a story based on my childhood, I wasn't sure how or where to begin. I was surprised that my thoughts kept coming back to a long-forgotten episode involving a kitten I found one summer when I was ten. Slowly, the events and feelings came into sharper focus—and while I can't swear that every moment of this story really happened, I know that every feeling is true. And in time, I came to understand that the reason for writing this story had less to do with the kitten and more to do with my brothers and myself.

As I was the youngest, my three brothers were very important in my thinking about who I was and who I would be when I grew up. All my brothers were interested in the arts and at one time or another planned on arts-related careers. As it turned out, I was the only one who actually realized that particular dream.

But my entire family was instrumental in my becoming a writer. We were a word-loving family. Our house was full of books and games; no dinner conversation was complete without jokes and wordplay. My mother recognized my talent as a writer early on and encouraged me to consider it as a profession. It took me a long time to follow her advice, but when I did, it was like coming home. Writing has always been a natural part of who I am."

Katherine Paterson

WHY I NEVER RAN AWAY FROM HOME

✳

KATHERINE PATERSON

My daughter Mary doesn't like for me to tell this story. "It's too sad," she says. "It was a sad time," I say. "I'm very happy now." "But I want my mommy to be happy when she's little," she says. "It has a happy ending," I say. "It tells why I never ran away from home."

"Guess what?" That's all my nine-year-old sister Lizzie had to say to get me excited.

"What?"

"You'll never guess," Lizzie said. And I wouldn't. Lizzie was too smart for me. She'd skipped second grade, the one I was stumbling through. Everyone praised Lizzie. Momma depended on her to help with our two baby sisters. Complete strangers would stop Momma to say how pretty Lizzie was. "Such darling freckles," they'd say. Lizzie would frown. She didn't think freckles were darling, but I did. I wanted to be just like Lizzie. Smart, dependable, pretty. Even our brother Sonny thought she was terrific, and Sonny was twelve years old.

"What?" I asked again. "What? What? Tell me."

"We're going to see a moving picture show. The mothers are going to take us into Shanghai to see *The Wizard of Oz*." Lizzie knew all about *The Wizard of Oz*. She'd read the book.

We lived in China when I was seven, and I'd never seen a movie. Well, actually, I had seen part of one, but I got scared and began crying so loud that Momma had to take me out before it was half over.

"You mustn't yell this time," Lizzie warned. "You'll ruin it for everyone."

"Okay," I promised, already thrilled and scared.

"If it gets too scary for you, you can close your eyes, and I'll punch you when it's okay to watch again, all right?"

I nodded solemnly and promised myself that no matter what happened I would not cry. I knew Lizzie thought I was a crybaby. I was born on Halloween, so she and Sonny often called me "Spook Baby." They could count on me to burst into tears every time they did. If I called Lizzie "Lizard," she'd ignore me or just look at me and laugh.

As excited as I was about going to see *The Wizard of Oz*, I was frightened by the trip into the city. True, there

Katherine Paterson

52

were no bombs falling, no enemy soldiers standing about with guns and bayonets as there were in other Chinese cities where we'd lived. But Shanghai beyond the safe walls of the American School was crowded with desperate people.

Outside the school gate, the mothers herded our little group of American children into rickshas to go to the theater. While they did so, Chinese children no bigger than I was crowded around us. These children wore rags for clothes. I could see that their faces and bodies were covered with sores, as they pushed their dirty hands at my face, begging for coins.

I wished for my Daddy. I was never as frightened when our tall, funny father was with us. But all the fathers were far away. Ours was back home with our Chinese friends in Hwaian, near the worst of the fighting. I knew I was supposed to be happy that God needed Daddy there working with Pastor Lee to help people who were hungry and hurt by the war. But I wasn't happy; I was jealous of those people. I wanted Daddy to be with us.

Once the movie began, though, I was swallowed up in its magic. The real world of war and homesickness and fear seemed to disappear. Even I was changed. I was no longer an ordinary-looking seven-year-old crybaby. In my soul, I knew that I looked exactly like Judy Garland.

True, I missed a lot of the cyclone, most of the flying monkeys, and only got a few deliciously scary glimpses of the Wicked Witch of the West. But Lizzie kept her promise. She poked me when it was safe to watch again, so I didn't miss too much of the movie, and I only cried after Dorothy was safely home in Kansas.

The management was selling phonograph albums of the music in the theater lobby. Patty Jean White's mother bought one. I longed to have one for my own, but the White's dormitory room was right near ours. Surely Patty Jean would let the rest of us listen. Besides, we'd lost our record player when the soldiers looted our house in Hwaian.

For the next several days, the seven of us who had seen the movie gathered in the Whites' room and listened to the record. I loved those songs, especially "Somewhere Over the Rainbow." I longed to go over the rainbow. It sounded more like heaven than the place we sang hymns about every day and twice on Sundays. Besides, when I sang that song, I knew I sounded just like Judy Garland.

"Let's play Oz," Lizzie said one day while we were listening.

We looked at her in astonishment. "There's no room," someone said.

"Not indoors, silly. Outdoors in the quadrangle." We got excited. The Shanghai American School buildings surrounded a rectangle of huge green lawn. The quadrangle would make a wonderful Land of Oz.

"I'll be Dorothy," I offered.

Everyone turned and stared. "I'm supposed to be Dorothy," I said, a bit anxiously. Couldn't they see I was born to be Dorothy? Besides, I knew all the words. I was getting more agitated. Couldn't they understand? No one could sing those songs with more feeling.

Lizzie was the first one to speak up. "No," she said. "And stop jumping up and down. Patty Jean will be Dorothy. She has the right hair."

It wasn't fair. Patty Jean was an only child. Her mother had nothing better to do than brush and braid her long blonde hair. No one ever brushed my short brown hair but me, and I usually forgot.

"You have to be pretty to be Dorothy." Lizzie continued. Patty Jean began to priss up her mouth at that. "Besides—" and this was the worst blow of all—"besides," Lizzie said, "Patty Jean can sing."

I was crushed. I could imagine one of the other kids saying something that mean, but my very own sister? She and Sonny could laugh at me in our room, but right in front of everybody? I was working so hard at not crying that before I knew it, all the good parts were gone.

"You're small for your age," Lizzie was saying. "You can be a Munchkin."

"Lizard," I muttered under my breath. "Lizard. Lizard. Lizard." Lizzie pretended not to hear me.

I wanted to complain to Momma when we went back

to our room that afternoon, but Sonny was visiting, playing with the little girls so Momma could write Daddy a letter. Even with Sonny staying in the big boys' dormitory, our room was so crowded with beds that you could hardly walk around them.

Sitting on her bed writing, Momma looked worried. She always looked worried in those days, especially when she was writing to Daddy. Would he be hurt out there where the war was going on? Would he be killed? Would we ever see him again?

If my mother was worried, I was terrified. What would I do without my wise father? I was terribly home-sick for him. I wrote letters to him whenever I could. We were never sure he would get our letters, but we sent them anyway.

"I'm going to write a letter to Daddy," I announced, as soon as I realized that no one was in a mood to listen to me whine. I slid across the bed on my knees to look over Momma's shoulder. I liked to copy the grown-up way my mother wrote. "Lovingly, Mary." That's the way she signed her letters.

"Look at this!" Lizzie yelled when I proudly showed her the letter I had written. She made her way between the beds to show it to Sonny. Sonny snorted. They both laughed.

"Give it to me," I said, trying to grab back my letter. But they passed it back and forth over my head.

Momma tried to get them to calm down. "But, Momma," Lizzie said. "Look how she signed it!"

"I signed it just like Momma does."

"No you didn't. You said 'Lovely Katherine.' Lovely Katherine," she repeated, her voice ending in a squeak. Then she and Sonny doubled over in hysterical laughter. Even Momma was trying hard not to smile.

For a while, Lizzie and Sonny called me "Lovely Katherine" instead of "Spook Baby." I tried not to cry, but I couldn't help it. It was mean of them. I knew that no one thought I was lovely. Momma was lovely. Lizzie was lovely. Even prissy Patty Jean was lovely. I was a Munchkin.

I was, as it turned out, the only Munchkin. I did my best. I sang "Follow the Yellow Brick Road" through my nose as loud as I could, hoping that Susan or Margaret (I'd given up on Lizzie) would take note of my superior acting ability and promote me to a better role. It didn't work. Not only did I not get a promotion, I didn't even get a solo. After a few bars, the older girls decided that it was stupid to have just one Munchkin singing. I would *be* the Munchkin, but everyone would have to help with singing "Follow the Yellow Brick Road."

So they all sang with me, but when Patty Jean, with her stuffed bear that played Toto, and Susan and Margaret and Billy left Munchkinland, my career as Munchkin was over.

"What am I supposed to do now?" I asked, ever hopeful.

"Sit down and be the audience," said Margaret. I looked to Lizzie, but she had forgotten me. She was having a wonderful time. She was the Wicked Witch. She even had a costume. She'd tied Momma's purple shawl around her shoulders like a cape. There were no trees in the middle of the quadrangle to hide behind, but Lizzie didn't need trees. She huddled on the ground, completely hidden by her witch cape. She lay still for a long time, waiting until the others were in the middle of a song or deep in conversation about the wonders of Oz and then *POOF!* she leaped right into their path, cackling away. Everyone would jump and scream each time as though it had never happened before.

That gave me an idea. Wouldn't it be great—just when the four friends plus stuffed bear were most downhearted—wouldn't it be great to have a friendly Munchkin poof into the action? Surely the magical appearance of a Munchkin would cheer them up and send them on down the yellow brick road with renewed courage.

"Don't forget!" I cried, bursting into a nasal song. "You're off to see the wizard—the wonderful—" The Scarecrow, Lion, and Tin Man dragged me out of their path back to the audience spot (I was also the entire audience) and sat me down. Lizzie just stood there and watched without saying a word. I could see the smirk on Patty Jean's face, which proved how unworthy she was to play Dorothy. Judy Garland would never smirk at a humiliated Munchkin.

I didn't cry. Only babies cried, and babies weren't allowed to play with the big kids. If I dared cry, I would be sent to play with the little ones.

I can't remember how many weeks our chief entertainment was *The Wizard of Oz,* but eventually Lizzie and the others tired of it. Besides, the big boys of our families had started a new game.

During the day, workmen were digging a trench across the wide green quadrangle to install new pipes. When we left the school dining room after supper, it was not quite dusk. Sonny and some of his friends invented a game called "Snake in the Gutter." One of the twelve-year-olds, the bigger the better, would be the snake. Everyone else would have to jump across the ditch while the snake ran up and down trying to grab you. If the snake touched you, you were dead.

I had thought anything would be better than being a Munchkin, but I was wrong. At least there was music and imagination and longing in that game. In Snake in the Gutter, there was only twilight terror and certain death. Patty Jean's mother took one look and refused to let her darling play. I sneered at that. The ditch was only two feet deep and about that wide. And it wasn't really dark. But without Patty Jean in the game, I was the youngest, the slowest player. Every night, I was always the first to be caught and killed.

One day that spring, Lizzie and I came back to our dorm room after school to find a lady we didn't know visiting with Momma. There was no room for chairs, of course, so the women were each sitting on the edge of a bed. As usual, Momma had the two little ones falling off her lap onto the bed beside her. She introduced Lizzie and me to her visitor as her two older daughters. I hardly had time to be proud that I was one of the older ones when the woman started looking us up and down as though she was shopping for a piece of furniture.

Finally, she smiled at Lizzie. "Isn't she lovely," she said. "What charming freckles." Then she turned and stared at me again. "Now, Mary," she said, "you can't tell me this one belongs to you. She doesn't look a bit like the rest of the family." She laughed as though she had said something funny. "Where on earth did you pick up this little stranger?"

My mother was sputtering in protest. She reached out and put an arm around me, but it didn't help. I had heard the visitor's pronouncement, not my mother's denial. So that was it. My parents had adopted me, but my mother was too kind to tell me that I wasn't really theirs. It seemed to explain everything—why my mother hardly had time even to brush my hair, why Lizzie wouldn't take up for me in front of the others, why I wasn't beautiful like my mother or clever like my father . . .

That night, after the snake bit me, I just started to walk away. It wasn't worth the fight. I wasn't thinking about what lay in the gathering darkness outside the walls of the school—war, crime, beggar children with their dirty hands stretched out—that was all forgotten. I was leaving.

I got to the edge of the quadrangle, nearly to the gate, when suddenly I realized that Lizzie had left the game and was chasing after me. When she caught up, she was panting from running so hard.

"Where do you think you're going?" she demanded, holding her side while she tried to catch her breath.

"I'm running away," I said. I felt perfectly calm. I hadn't considered for a moment that when you run away, you need some place to run to. I was just walking out.

"What do you mean, 'running away'?" She grabbed my arm. She was clearly angry. "It's nearly dark out there."

"I know," I said, shaking off her hand. "I don't care." I started walking again.

"Don't be stupid," she said.

"I'm not stupid," I said calmly. "But it's no use staying here. Nobody likes me, and I know I'm adopted, but Momma's too nice to tell me."

Lizzie really grabbed me now. She whirled me

around, and although it was nearly night, I could see fire in her eyes. "You can't run away. I won't let you. And if you even try, I will never speak to you again as long as you live."

Since that night, many people have told me that they loved me, but perhaps never quite so effectively. I thought about running away off and on for several years after that, but I would immediately discard the notion. After all, I couldn't run away. Lizzie wouldn't let me. It was a very comforting thought.

Notes from
KATHERINE PATERSON

"When I tried to think of a story to tell for this collection, I was nearly stumped. I could remember plenty of anecdotes from my past, but a real story with a beginning, middle, and end seemed hard to come by. The story I have told seemed closest to having a plot, but there was a problem: It was as much my older sister's story as my own—what if she hated it?

With fear and trembling, I sent Elizabeth

(we now call her Liz, not Lizzie) a copy of what I'd written. She wrote me back a postcard. 'Not to worry,' she said. 'I liked it.' Whew! But if you've read the story, you already know what a great person Lizzie is and aren't the least bit surprised that she's still helping her little sister through frightening situations.

Although I loved to read and often fantasized about growing up to be powerful and famous, it never occurred to me as a child that someday I would be a writer. In the sixth grade I did achieve a measure of fame as a dramatist. I wrote plays that my friends and I practiced during recess and were occasionally allowed to act out for the class. Creative writing wasn't a part of 'real schoolwork' in those days. Writing meant penmanship—dipping your pen into the inkwell and inscribing loops and slants on the page. Since I nearly always dropped a large blob of indelible ink on the paper, my grades in writing tended to be poor.

It wasn't until I was in college that my professors suggested that I might have some writing talent. I didn't take the idea seriously until after I was married and had the first of our four children."

Walter Dean Myers

REVEREND ABBOTT AND THOSE BLOODSHOT EYES

WALTER DEAN MYERS

When I was a kid in the late forties, I thought the whole world was like Harlem, full of life and colors and music that spilled out onto the streets for all the people to enjoy. Life was a constant adventure, although some moments were a lot more adventuresome than others. Take, for example, the fight between the kids on our block and Reverend Abbott, our visiting minister. We didn't have anything against Reverend Abbott because he was white, and I don't think he had anything against us because we weren't. In fact, he was probably a good man, and I'm sure he didn't deserve to have so much trouble during his first summer serving the Lord.

Reverend Robinson, our regular minister, was away for the summer trying to raise money for the church's upstate camp, Rabbit Hollow. That left Reverend Abbott just about in charge, or at least he thought he was.

Actually, if Reverend Abbott hadn't tried so hard to help us, things might have been different. Take the time he tried to protect us from Sugar Ray Robinson, the greatest fighter in the world. We used to play a game called Skullies. You drew numbered boxes in the middle of the street and you shot bottle caps or checkers from one number to the other until you became a "killer," and then you knocked out all the other bottle caps. One day, about four of us were really involved in a game of Skullies and didn't notice the long, almost pink Cadillac cruising down the street. The driver of the Caddy was Sugar Ray Robinson, welterweight champion of the world. In those days, a lot of athletes either lived in or hung out in Harlem. Sugar Ray would often come around and play with the kids, the same way that Willie Mays, the baseball all-star, did when he came to New York.

OK, so Sugar Ray yelled at us, asking why we were blocking his car. Then he got out and challenged us to a fight. Now, we knew that Sugar Ray Robinson was the welterweight champion and would not hurt any of us, but Reverend Abbott didn't know anything of the sort. All he saw was a man getting out of his car and challenging the kids. He came out yelling at Sugar Ray and telling him that he had better get back into his car.

Sugar Ray took one look at the tall, thin man in front of him, shook his head, and got back into his Caddy.

We tried to explain to Reverend Abbott that you didn't jump up into the face of Sugar Ray, but he didn't seem to get it. He just kept insisting that fighting was wrong and that we should learn to turn the other cheek. It was clear to us that the good reverend was trying to mess things up for us.

Being a kid in Harlem wasn't the easiest way to live. We didn't have much of a crime problem in those days, but we did have to worry about the Window Watchers and the Root Ladies. We certainly didn't need anybody else to look out for.

The Window Watchers were the biggest pain because there were more of them. They were the women who used to bring their pillows to the windows and watch what was happening on the block. Sometimes they would talk to each other from the windows, or order up collard greens from the vegetable man who brought his truck around in the afternoons. But mostly, they would watch what was going on and report to your mother if you did anything they considered wrong.

I remember one time Johnny Lightbourne threw a candy wrapper on the sidewalk in front of the church. A Window Watcher spotted him from the fourth floor and called down to another Watcher on the first floor. Johnny's mother knew about it before he got home.

This was bad, but the Root Ladies were worse. The thing was, you didn't mess with Root Ladies. Not that you actually believed that they could do anything with their roots and candles and mumbo jumbo, but there was no use taking chances. When you went over to La Marketa, you saw them sitting with rows of colored candles and twisted little roots that Fat Butch said looked like dried-up shrunken people, and you saw that they looked a little strange, and you crossed the street. No big deal—unless somebody threw a snowball at one of them and they looked at you with the evil eye. All you had to do if a Root Lady gave you the evil eye was to hold up a mirror and shine it back at her. You had to know how to protect yourself when you were a kid. In a cigar box in my closet, I kept a small mirror for Root Ladies, a crucifix for vampires, and a ground-up peach pit to throw on dogs with purple tongues.

You also had to know some of the rules. You didn't play handball against a Root Lady's house, walk in her shadow, or bring a broom near her. If you followed the rules, you didn't have to worry—even if she could make her eyes glow and send them out at night to get you just when you were about ready to fall asleep.

What the Watchers and the Root Ladies did like was that all of the kids in the neighborhood went to church. In fact, most of our lives were centered around the church. I started Sunday school at about four and received my first book, *Stories for Every Day of the Year*, as a prize in the Tots Parade when I was five. In the summers, we went to Bible school, which was more like a summer camp than a religious school. Every kid in the neighborhood had made a wallet in Bible school.

We also learned to play basketball in the church gym. The ceiling in the gym was low and you could tell who played ball in our church because they had flat jump shots. The church also had dances for teenagers, and that really seemed to upset Reverend Abbott.

The dances had chaperones who carried fans advertising local funeral parlors. The chaperones would go through the crowd and put the fans between the couples dancing and tell them to "make room for the Holy Ghost."

When Reverend Abbott saw his first dance and the thirteen-and-up crowd doing their thing, he was upset. There was no room for such goings-on in the Presbyterian church. So he made an announcement that there would be no more dances while he was in charge. What he wanted to do was to substitute relay races and Bible quizzes for the dances. We didn't have MTV in those days, or video game arcades, and the dances were about our only social event. Somebody suggested a compromise: We would have relay races and square dancing. Reverend Abbott was pleased.

The next Friday was the first square dance. The chaperones stayed on the small stage and looked on approvingly. Then Reverend Abbott went to his study, and somebody put on a mambo record. It was hard to tell exactly who had put on the mambo record because it went on a second after the lights went out. The chaperones, mostly mothers and big sisters, immediately started for the light switches. They weren't that upset. But when Reverend Abbott opened the door and saw a host of healthy young bodies swinging to a frantic Latin beat in the eerie dimness of the red emergency lights, he was beside himself. The names of all the teenagers present were taken and their parents were notified the next morning by a committee of church ladies.

OK, so Reverend Abbott wanted a fight. We decided to give him one.

We had had young ministers like Reverend Abbott before. They would work for a few months in the church, then go on to another area or, if they were lucky, to their own church. We found out that Reverend Abbott was scheduled to give his first sermon on the second Sunday after breaking up our dance.

We also found out that there was going to be an important funeral in the church later that same day. Sam Johnson, the numbers man and Bar-B-Que King of Eighth Avenue, had died. Mr. Johnson was famous for his girth, his gold tooth, his promptness in paying off when you hit the number, and his barbecue sauce. It was rumored that his funeral would be attended by every big-time gangster in Harlem. There would even be, the story went, some Italian gangsters from East Harlem coming over.

So Reverend Abbott was going to have not one but two chances to show his stuff: He would give the morning sermon at 9:30 and then conduct the funeral at 12:00. He wanted to get them both right. Several sisters said that whenever they passed the minister's study, he was either sweating over his message or down on his knees, praying. It was to be his big day.

It was going to be our big day too.

The kids were divided into two groups—the "littles," of which I was one, and the teenagers. It was the teenagers who came up with the plan to undermine Reverend Abbott. But the littles were part of the plot.

Sunday school started in our church at 8:00 and was over at 8:45. At 9:15, the recorded caroling bells would start, calling all the worshipers to Sunday morning service.

At 9:00, Reverend Abbott was in his study, making last-minute changes in his sermon. Girls with ribbons on their braids and Vaseline rubbed into their faces and knees were out in front of the church. Some of the boys were planning to go to the West End Theater, which was showing three features and a serial. But some of the littles knew what was going to happen, and one of them had already sneaked upstairs and found out that it was Mrs. Davis who was going to put on the record that would summon everyone to church. Her favorite hymn was "What a Friend We Have in Jesus," and its version of recorded bells sounded very nice. The little who discovered Mrs. Davis in the sound room went out and relayed the message to the big kids.

At three minutes to nine, the telephone on the first floor rang. There was a breathless voice on the wire: an urgent message for Mrs. Davis. Mrs. Davis was a pillar of the church. A tall woman with broad shoulders, a wide, dark face, and eyes that turned up ever so slightly, she had been one of its earliest members. Now she was being called downstairs with the word *emergency* ringing in her ears.

Emergencies in those days did not mean that your cat was in a tree or your car had a flat. An emergency in Harlem meant one of two things, either a death in the family or a fire.

Mrs. Davis rushed from the sound room, grasping the railings heavily as she made her way down the stairs toward the first floor telephone. The sound of her feet on the steps could be heard all the way down the hall.

Much to her surprise, there was no one on the phone when she answered it.

The sneakers on the teenager who ran into the sound room could hardly be heard. The record on the player was removed and another put in its place. The volume was turned up slightly. The door was closed and a padlock was put in place—not, mind you, the same padlock that was usually there and for which Mrs. Davis still held the key in her hands.

Then the teenager disappeared on his sneakered feet, down the stairs and out the side door onto 122nd Street.

The record could be heard all over the neighborhood. *"OOOOOO-EE! DON'T ROLL YOUR BLOOD-SHOT EYES AT ME!"*

Heads turned, mouths dropped opened, eyes widened. People couldn't believe what they were hearing!

The lyrics were less than elegant. The song, about a man who had been out all night carousing and whose eyes are bloodshot in the morning, wasn't that original. But coming from the church sound system, amplified for the glory of God and the amusement of the entire neighborhood, it would long be remembered.

Reverend Abbott himself flew up the stairs, two at a time, sweat popping off his brow, only to find the heavy door hopelessly locked.

Mrs. Davis followed to find him banging on the padlock with his fist. She took a look, saw the padlock had been changed, and turned and rushed back down the stairs in search of the church janitor.

The record played over and over until the janitor was located and the lock broken. By the time the record was removed and the proper one put on in its place, the entire church was in an uproar. Some people were upset, and others suppressed smiles. We littles went into the back alley and told each other what records we would have put on if we had had the chance. We also stuck our fingers with a pin and swore in blood that we wouldn't tell who had done it, even though only a few of us knew which teenager had actually been in the sound room.

Reverend Abbott started his sermon by talking about how some people didn't realize how lucky they were to have a nice church like ours. Then he tried to get into his regular sermon, which was about all the work that Noah put in when he built the ark and why we should all work for God. But he was so nervous that he forgot most of it.

The funeral went a lot better. Because Fat Butch's mama was Sam Johnson's goddaughter, he had to go to the funeral with her. He said that Reverend Abbott went on about how it wasn't always easy to tell a good man from a bad man and how we shouldn't judge people without seeing their true hearts. All the gangsters at the funeral liked this a lot and one even cried.

The next Sunday, Reverend Abbott put two teenagers in charge of making sure the right record was on, which stopped all the hopes of the littles that "Open the Door, Richard" would call the faithful to church.

On Reverend Abbott's last Sunday, he thanked the congregation and said that he thought he was ready to face any challenge that God might put before him. He was probably right.

Notes from
WALTER DEAN MYERS

"When I was a child, I was too busy working at childhood to notice if I was having a good time of it or not. In thinking back, it seems as if I must have enjoyed myself most of the time. Judging from what was important to me— Stoop Ball, Kick-the-Can, Scullies, and other games—it's clear that I wasn't worried that my family was poor, which we were, or about neighborhood violence.

As a young boy, I belonged to the Presbyterian church on the corner of my block, and the church and its teachings belonged to me as well. The church was just an extension of our homes, or so it seemed. We drew our values, and our strengths, from that community and that church. It told us that life was good, and so were we. I'd like to recapture that feeling for young people today.

The church has traditionally played an important part in the lives of African Americans, both for regular churchgoers and for the community at large. Many activities—religious, social, and at some times, political—had their beginnings and often their focal point in the church. Our leadership came most often from the pulpit as well. Consider Martin Luther King, Jr., or Malcolm X, or Adam Clayton Powell—all ministers, all leaders.

My grandfather was a great storyteller. He could bring his stories, almost all taken from the Old Testament, to life in a way that would make me tremble. My stepfather used to tell stories too. His were usually scary stories, and sometimes funny. Like my stepdad and my grandfather, I tell stories too, only I write mine down."

Susan Cooper

MUFFIN

~⚞~

SUSAN COOPER

When a war has been going on for more than a third of your life, you feel it's always been there. It seemed normal, to the children of Cippenham Primary School, that there were air-raid shelters on the school playground, long, windowless concrete buildings half sunk into the ground, and that they should all sit inside, singing songs or reciting multiplication tables, whenever the bombers came rumbling their deadly way overhead. It seemed normal that every signpost in the country should have been removed; normal that the streets were fringed with huge concrete barriers called "tank traps," to make life difficult for the invading enemy if the Germans should ever manage to cross the English Channel.

Daisy and her friends took all this for granted, like the fact that they'd never seen a fountain or a steak or a banana. They didn't recognize that they were living through World War II; it was just "the war." It was part of life.

Fat Alice was part of life too, unfortunately. She was the boss of the school playground: a big, pasty-faced girl with short straight hair and an incongruously shrill voice. A group of hangers-on drifted in her wake, notably Pat and Maggie, two wispy, wiry girls who hovered about her like pilot fish escorting a shark. As prey for her little gang, Fat Alice chose a particular victim at the beginning of each term. This term she had chosen Daisy.

It was a Monday morning in a blossoming spring, but Alice, Pat, and Maggie were not paying attention to the daffodils. The three of them had Daisy cornered against the fence just inside the playground gate. It was a rough wooden fence, put up to replace the elegant old wrought-iron railings that had been taken away for the War Effort, to be melted down and used for guns, or ammunition, or bombs. A splinter drove deep into Daisy's arm, where it was pushed against the wood by Maggie's mean little fingers.

"Ow!" said Daisy. "Ow-ow-ow!"

"Shut up," said Fat Alice, in her high, whiny voice. "Walk along the line like I said, and don't step off it or you'll get punished."

Fear was making Daisy breathe fast. She felt sick. She teetered along the chalk line they had drawn on the ground, and because of her fear she lost her balance, and lurched to one side. Shrieking with delight, the other three fell on her, pulling her blonde braids, shoving her to the ground so that Fat Alice could grab her hand and scrape the back of it over the gravel-studded asphalt. This was Alice's favorite torture; she had learned it from her brother, who ruled the boys' end of the playground.

Daisy squealed. Her hand was bleeding. She aimed a furious kick at Fat Alice's bulging leg as her three tormentors scattered, and the kick was seen by Mrs. Walker, one of the "dinner ladies" who not only served meals but also kept watch during recess, to prevent the children of Cippenham Primary School from murdering each other. "Daisy Morgan!" screeched Mrs. Walker. "I seen that! No kicking! I'll tell your teacher!"

But a dog was barking fiercely on the other side of the fence, a little gray terrier with sharp-pricked ears and tail, and beside him stood the old lady who lived in the house next to the school. Daisy didn't know her name. She was standing very upright, wearing a shapeless brown cardigan and skirt, and she was shaking her stick at Mrs. Walker.

"It wasn't the girl's fault!" she called, in a clear, authoritative voice. "She was defending herself! I saw the others attacking her!"

The bell rang, and Daisy fled for school. Mrs. Walker sniffed suspiciously as she passed, but she didn't report her.

At dinnertime, Daisy slid a piece of meat from her

plate into her handkerchief, even though it was—for once—good-tasting meat instead of rubbery gristle, and she hid it in her pocket. On the way home after school, she paused by the fence.

The old lady and her dog were standing on their doorstep like sentries, watching the shouting hundreds of children flood untidily by. Daisy called out, "Please may I give him a piece of meat?"

"I'm sure he'd be delighted," the old lady said in her strong clear voice. "Muffin! Show your manners!"

Muffin barked, twice, deliberately, before bolting the limp gray square that Daisy tossed to him. Beaming, Daisy waved, and ran home.

"Alice Smith did it," she said, sitting at the kitchen table, wincing as her mother dabbed antiseptic on her scraped hand. "Alice Smith is a *Nazi!*"

Daisy's mother spent most of her time worrying about Daisy's father, who was in a destroyer somewhere in the North Atlantic, chasing enemy submarines. She said softly, "I don't think so, darling. Not quite."

But Alice and Pat and Maggie were on the attack again next day at recess, chasing Daisy into a corner and lashing at her bare legs with thin whippy branches torn from the old lady's front hedge. Daisy heard Muffin barking indignantly at them and knew that the old lady was watching, but she was running too fast to be able to ask for help. Instead she took the perilous step of complaining to her teacher about her persecution. Her teacher spoke reproachfully to Fat Alice for thirty seconds, and Fat Alice sat next to Daisy in the shelter during the next air-raid practice and pinched her silently and viciously for half an hour.

Daisy's arm was black and blue. She felt desperate. There was no escape. All her life she was going to be made miserable by the Alice gang, and nothing she did could make the slightest difference. After school that day, on a wild impulse, she ran down the sidewalk and in through the old lady's front gate. Beside the front door, a forsythia bush was blooming like a great yellow cloud.

Daisy knocked at the door. "Please," she said when it opened, "please—" and to her horror she burst into tears.

"Oh dear," said the old lady. "This won't do. Come in and have a cup of tea with Muffin and me."

It was a house filled with framed old-fashioned photographs and hundreds of small ornaments; it felt friendly. Muffin lay with his chin across Daisy's feet. Over a cup of comforting weak tea with milk and sugar, and two digestive biscuits, Daisy asked the old lady if she would mind speaking to her teacher, to describe what she had seen Fat Alice do. If a grown-up gave witness, perhaps there was a chance the tormenting might stop.

"Of course I will!" the old lady said briskly. "Bullies must always be stopped, by any means possible. That's what this war is all about. I shall speak to your teacher tomorrow."

But before the morning came, the village of Cippenham was given a very noisy night. Daisy was woken in the darkness, as so often before, by the chilling up-and-down wail of the air-raid siren, agitating the night from a loudspeaker on the roof of the local police station. She pulled on her raincoat over her pajamas, slung her gas-mask case over her shoulder, and followed her mother and her sleepy four-year-old brother Mike out to their air-raid shelter, the little turf-roofed, metal-walled cave sunk into the back lawn. The night was cold, and the bright beams of searchlights groped to and fro over the dark sky. There was already a faint rumble of aircraft engines in the air.

"Quickly, darlings!" Her mother hurried them to the shelter door, behind its barricade of sandbags. It was hard to see anything; flashlights were forbidden in the blacked-out nights of wartime England, where the windows of every house were covered closely by black curtains, or by strips of sticky brown tape that would also keep glass from scattering if the windows were blown in by blast.

Daisy could hear shells bursting in the sky, fired from the long guns of the anti-aircraft post at the end of the street. Then the bombs began falling, with their unmistakable dull *crump* sound, vibrating through the earth.

She had never been much afraid of the bombs, not with the intense personal terror she felt when Fat Alice and her friends jumped out at her. But this time, the bombs sounded closer than ever before—a sequence of huge crashes, louder and louder, shaking the shelter so that the single lighted candle jumped and flickered on the earthen floor. Daisy buried her head in her mother's lap.

It was a long night, before the single steady note of the all clear sang out through the sky, and they could go back to bed.

When Daisy set out from home next morning, she found a crowd of excited children milling in the road near her school, and behind them a fluttering orange tape strung as a temporary barrier across the road. Behind the tape was a huge hole. Broken pipes jutted from the clay-brown soil; the earth had been sliced as if it were a cake.

"What is it?" Daisy said to the nearest familiar face.

"It's a bomb crater, stupid! Jeff found three super bits of shrapnel!"

"A whole stick of bombs fell last night." This was a chunky, confident boy called Fred, who always came top of Daisy's class. "Our two were the first, that's why they're closer together."

"Our two?" Daisy said.

"The other one's right by the playground. Just our luck it didn't hit school."

"Jerry can't shoot straight!"

"Look, there's all the teachers! They're sending every-one home!"

Daisy wasn't listening. She was edging along what was left of the sidewalk, past the crater, past houses whose windows were blank and empty, their glass all blown in by the bomb. Assorted grown-ups frowned at her and called her back, but not before she had reached the playground gate—splintered now, and hanging from one hinge. She saw the playground littered with bricks and broken glass and strange pieces of metal. And beside it, she saw an unfamiliar gap. The old lady's house was no longer there.

Daisy rushed forward, into the playground, ignoring the shouts behind her, until she stood at the edge of the ruin where the house had been. It was a mass of rubble, of broken brick and splintered beams; she saw a piece of carpet jutting from underneath a pile of roofing tiles. There was a strong smell of dust.

A hand took hold of her shoulder; it was the elderly policeman who watched the road crossing before and after school.

"Come on, love. You can't come here—it's dangerous."

"The old lady," Daisy said urgently. She looked up at him. "The old lady?"

"Did you know her?" said the policeman.

"Sort of," Daisy said.

The policeman hesitated, then sighed. "She was killed by the bomb. Direct hit. She can't have known a thing about it."

Daisy stared at him, stunned. Yesterday the old lady had given her tea and digestive biscuits. Today she didn't exist. It wasn't possible.

The policeman said again, gently, "Come on."

As Daisy turned to go with him, a movement in the ruins of the house caught her eye. She paused, peering, and saw Muffin, cowering behind a heap of rubble. He seemed to be unhurt, but he was coated with dust and dirt, and he was shivering—shaking all over, violently, as if he were terribly cold.

"Muffin! Here, boy! Muffin!" She tried to get his attention, but he wouldn't look at her. She wondered if he could hear.

"It's the bomb," the policeman said. "That her dog, is it? England's full of dogs and cats like that, these days. Lost their people. Shell-shocked, like. Come on then, boy!" He moved toward the dog, hand outstretched, but Muffin turned away abruptly and fled.

"We'll keep an eye out for him," the policeman said.

Before she went home, Daisy stopped at the tiny general store opposite the school. Its windows had all been blown in, but it was still open; indeed there was a cheerful notice lettered on the plywood which had already been nailed over the windowframe, reading:

MORE OPEN THAN USUAL. With some pennies she found in her pocket, Daisy bought a bun, and when nobody was looking she threw it into the ruins of the old lady's house. Muffin would be back, and he would be hungry.

And Muffin did come back. Before long, the playground was cleared of rubble, the road was repaired, the remains of the old lady's house were flattened, and school began again. And the children began to notice Muffin, sometimes, lying on the ground where his house had been. He was thin and dirty, and his ears and tail were no longer as perky as they had been before. Some of the children tried to call him, or catch him, but he always ran away.

Only once, when Daisy was alone and called, "Muffin! Muffin! Show your manners!"—then Muffin came trotting to her and licked her hand, and let her pat him. But even then he leaped away when she tried to take hold of his collar. There was no sign of him afterward, for days.

Fat Alice had been distracted from her usual pursuits by the excitement of the bomb craters, and the prestigious bits of shrapnel that could be collected, or taken away from the collections of smaller, weaker boys or girls. She had not forgotten Daisy, however. She began now a quiet campaign of small intermittent cruelties, with no reason or pattern. At unexpected times of the day, in classroom or playground or corridor, she would appear suddenly at Daisy's side and give her a quick fierce kick or pinch, vanishing afterward with a speed remarkable in one so large. Daisy began to feel constantly nervous, like a hunted animal.

Sometimes she felt angry with herself for doing nothing to combat the maliciousness of Alice Smith. But what was there to do? She was outsized and outnumbered, and the little gang of bullies took care never to do anything that might catch the attention of a teacher. Now that Daisy had lost the old lady, the only grown-up she could enlist as saviour was her mother. But that had been tried last term, by Molly Barnes, a placid, amiable girl even fatter than Alice, who was the butt of the gang for so long that she seemed to be constantly in tears. Molly's mother had come to school to complain—and close on her heels had come Alice's mother, a tough, aggressive lady who was heard, through the headmaster's closed door, angrily shouting a number of words Daisy had never heard uttered before.

So the headmaster had not known which mother to believe, and the reign of Fat Alice had gone on undisturbed. And Daisy said nothing that would bring her own mother to the school, because she knew the result would be just the same.

It was a Friday, four weeks after the bombs fell, when Alice did the worst thing of all. Daisy liked Fridays, not only because they marked the end of the week, but because the last class of the day was art. She loved drawing and painting, more than anything. Even though, in their overcrowded school, her class had to double up with Alice's class for art—giving Alice easy opportunities for poking Daisy with one end of a paintbrush, or dabbing paint on her skirt with the other—even so, it was Daisy's favorite class.

And this Friday was even better than most. Their teacher said, "Think of the best story you've ever heard from your mother or father, and paint me a picture of it."

Daisy thought of the last time her father had come home on leave, after he had been sailing to the north coast of Russia on what he called "the Murmansk run," and she painted what he had described. She painted his destroyer, as she often did at home, but she showed it encrusted all over with ice, with men muffled up in heavy jackets and gloves chipping the ice away from spars and guns and rails. She painted the gray angry sea and the big waves, and a patchy blue sky, and a huge, white jagged iceberg rearing up in the background. She particularly liked the iceberg.

"That's wonderful, Daisy!" said her teacher, and she held it up in front of the class. She said Daisy should take the picture home to show her mother, and then bring it back next week to be shown to the whole school in morning assembly.

Daisy set off cheerfully for home, in the noisy bouncing crowd pouring out of the playground. But a figure came running and pushed her sideways, and then another, and she found herself nudged and shoved out of sight of everyone else, behind the air-raid shelters. Alice, Pat, and Maggie closed around her, bright-eyed, grinning.

"She did *ever* such a nice painting!" said Alice, shrill, jeering. "She's so stuck-up, she thinks she's the cat's meow—here, I'll show you her *lovely* painting!"

She grabbed the rolled-up paper from under Daisy's arm.

"Give it back!" Daisy yelled. But Pat and Maggie were holding her arms, and she couldn't get free. She struggled, feeling her eyes blur with angry tears, and she saw Fat Alice unroll her beautiful painting and drop it deliberately face-down into a muddy puddle. Then Alice lifted her foot and trod on it.

Daisy let out a great sob, and kicked at Alice. She felt her shoe hit Alice's shinbone, hard.

Fat Alice shrieked with pain. Her face twisted with fury and venom, and she advanced on Daisy. "Just you wait!" she hissed.

But behind her, there was a sudden astounding noise, halfway between a roar and a shriek, and out of the wasteland that had been the old lady's house, Muffin came rushing. He looked very small, and very dangerous. He flung himself at Fat Alice, growling and snapping; then whirled at Pat and at Maggie, nipping their ankles, jumping up at them, teeth bared. A small dog had become a small tornado, a whirling flurry of danger and menace. The three girls screamed and backed away, but Muffin came after them, snarling, biting, until they scattered and ran.

"Mad dog!" Alice howled. "Mad dog . . ." Her voice faded as she disappeared down the road.

Muffin came back to Daisy. He looked up at her, panting, his tongue lolling, and she crouched beside him and fondled his small dirty head. Muffin licked her face.

"Let's go home, Muffin," Daisy said.

Muffin barked, deliberately, twice.

Daisy picked her painting out of the puddle. It was a blurred, muddy, unrecognizable mess. She crumpled it up and dropped it again, and she turned and ran out of the playground, through the streets, home. Muffin ran at her heels.

Bursting through the kitchen door, breathless, Daisy found her mother peeling potatoes. "Mum," she said, grasping for the words she had been rehearsing as she ran. "Mum, I have a friend, he's been bombed out, please can he stay?"

Daisy's mother looked down at Muffin.

"Dad says every ship should have a mascot," Daisy said.

Her mother smiled. She said, "You just have time to give him a bath before tea."

Notes from

SUSAN COOPER

"My story 'Muffin' is set in England during World War II, because that's where I was when I was your age. I once put all that part of my life into a book called *Dawn of Fear*, a war story which is pure autobiography except that I turned myself into a boy called Derek. Don't ask me why.

The main character in 'Muffin,' Daisy, is not me, but she goes to the same school as Derek/Susan, and the bombs that she hears fall are the same ones Derek hears in *Dawn of Fear*. I found myself wondering the other day whether Derek ever met Muffin. It's sometimes hard for writers to remember where real life ends and story begins.

I began life as a passionate reader and pretty soon realized I was a writer as well. When I edited my school magazine, I found it was much easier to write things than to persuade other people to write them, and I still own a rather embarrassing issue in which eleven contributions (and two pictures) are signed by Susan Cooper. I've been scribbling away ever since."

TAKING A DARE

⟍⟋

NICHOLASA MOHR

It all started the day my friend Casilda dared me. All my friends were hanging out in the schoolyard at St. Anselm's. It was around seven o'clock on Saturday evening. Casilda, Wanda, Mary, and little Ritchie had already confessed earlier.

Now we were just watching people leaving church after confessing. The kids began to talk about how confession made you feel different—pure and holy. ". . . so then the next day when you receive Communion," explained Casilda, "you become clean and without no sins." She looked up at the sky all dreamy-eyed, like she had just done something so perfect.

The fact was, all my friends—except for Joey who was Pentecostal—had already made their First Communion. Even little Ritchie, who was only eight, had made his Communion last year in Puerto Rico. I was ten years old and I still had not made my First Communion. Every Saturday, it was the same. Me and Joey had to wait until the rest of them confessed; then we had to hear how they all felt pure and terrific. More and more, I began to feel left out, like I was a stranger instead of their friend.

Here I was again, listening to them sound off. Blah, blah, and blah, bragging like they knew it all. I was really getting annoyed and decided to let them know just how I felt.

"It don't sound like a big deal to me," I told them.

"That's because you don't know what you are missing." Casilda went on boasting, paying me no mind. But I had already heard enough! I was going to show them what I thought of them and their holy selves.

"I think I'm gonna receive Holy Communion and without no confession," I blurted out.

"But you can't!" argued Wanda. "You have to go to confession and tell the priest all the bad things you done. Then the priest gives you prayers to say so that God will forgive your sins."

"That's right," added Mary. "That's called penance. You gotta say penance first to prepare for Holy Communion."

"Or else it's a sin—a big sin—and you could go to hell!" declared Casilda.

I enjoyed looking at their shocked expressions and decided to go even further. "But I don't believe in no confession. Anyway, my father says there ain't no hell and no heaven either. He says heaven and hell are right here on earth. Heaven is for the rich and hell is for the poor."

"That's a bad thing to say," shrieked Mary.

"You better not talk that way," warned Wanda.

"Yeah," agreed little Ritchie, "I think that's a real bad *sin* to say."

I just shrugged at their attempts to stop me. Actually, I was pleased to be getting all their attention.

"All right, since you act like it's no sin and you ain't scared, go on!" shouted Casilda loud and clear. "I dare you to receive Holy Communion tomorrow." I hesitated, but Casilda wouldn't let up. "Well Big Mouth, are you gonna do it or not?"

Everybody became quiet, waiting to see what I would do. So how could I back off? Especially the way Casilda got right into my face. No way was she going to make me look chicken in front of my friends.

"Well?" she shouted, standing with her hands on her hips and her chin pointing my way. "You said you were gonna do it. It's tomorrow or forget about it."

"Tomorrow for sure," I answered, trying to sound unconcerned and confident. "Unless you got a problem, girl, I'll see your face there too." I could hear the *oohs* and *aahs* from the others. But I stood my ground, because tomorrow at ten o'clock Mass, all my friends were coming to see me take Casilda's dare.

My mother blamed my attitude about religion and the

Catholic Church on my dad. And in more ways than one, she was right. You see, I never went to Catholic school like some of the other Catholic kids. The main reason was because we couldn't afford the fee. I was the youngest of seven children, and the only girl. Money was always scarce in our household. But even if we'd had the funds, my dad would have refused to pay for parochial school. He was an avid socialist and was opposed to organized religion, especially the Catholic Church.

So I was sent instead to catechism. Two afternoons a week I was let out early from public school to attend religious instruction at St. Anselm's Catholic school. But most of the time, I never got there like I was supposed to. Instead, I skipped catechism and played outside until it was time to go home. Or I'd go farther down to Third Avenue where the big stores were, and I'd window-shop.

When I did manage to attend catechism, I hardly paid attention. I found it all very boring. But now as I look back, I can see my dad's influence at work. "Don't be superstitious like your mother," he'd warn me. He told me to question everything the nuns taught me. My dad told me it was the bosses in our dominant society who wanted all workers to be obedient. Then the workers would never fight for justice or their rights. It was the Church's way, and the way of capitalism too, he told me.

When I asked him if he believed in God, he'd snap

back, "There is no God. There is humankind and only the here and now!"

He would never tell me these things in front of my mother. She was quite religious and always had a lit candle in a red glass holder in front of a holy picture of St. Lazarus. My mother often prayed at her small altar for the salvation of my father's soul.

But I wasn't so sure my dad was right. For instance, sometimes I'd sneak into St. Anselm's by myself, especially on the afternoons when I was supposed to be in religious instruction. If I heard or saw a priest, nun, or any grown-up, I would duck down behind one of the pews and remain out of sight.

I loved inhaling the fragrance of melted wax and incense. Sitting and just thinking in the silent, almost empty church had a comforting effect on me. Carefully, without making a sound, I would visit the stations of the cross and all the holy statues. I'd examine the details of each station and the carving of the snake beneath the sacred Virgin's feet. It was at once both mysterious and marvelous.

Occasionally, I tried to feel pious by staring at the faces of the large statues. I hoped to see them blink an eye or move a muscle. I waited for a signal that would prove their power. But they continued to stare blankly into space and never moved an inch. Still, I got to know each one and even developed a fondness for them. I had two favorites: the Sacred Heart of Jesus and the Immaculate Conception. I lit candles to them but never bothered to put a cent in the money box. Most of the time, I had no money. When I did get a few cents, it went to buying candy, which I was not about to give up for anybody or anything.

Whenever I was tempted to make a wish, I thought about my dad and felt like a traitor. I knew I was doing wrong by taking the candle in the first place. But since I didn't make a wish and asked for nothing, I figured it wasn't too terrible a sin.

But tomorrow, according to my friends, I *would* be committing a terrible sin. If my mom knew, she would surely give me a bad punishment. If I was caught, my dad wouldn't defend me either. For sure he'd say I got what was coming to me for playing silly games. No matter which way I figured it, I was risking deep trouble.

Besides, during my solo visits to St. Anselm's, I had bonded with my church. In fact, I figured how I probably knew it better than Casilda, Wanda, Mary, and her cousin Ritchie did! I knew each corner and just about every carving there. Even though I wasn't religious like my friends, I knew that the Communion wafer was supposed to be the body of Christ. Now *that* was a scary thought!

As much as I loved and respected both my parents, it was hard to figure out which one of them was right. I listened to my dad, but I also prayed just like my mom. Usually, I prayed to God. When I wanted something or got scared, I was not above pleading with God. I'd pray with all of my might: God let this happen or God don't let that happen. It seemed I always called on God when I needed help. During those times of need, prayers came naturally to me.

Tonight was no exception. I prayed real hard that something would happen to stop my going through with the dare. I also prayed that if I did go to church tomorrow, none of our neighbors would see me there, especially not nosy Mrs. Melendez. She was always watching out of her front window so she could gossip about everybody on our block. That whole night, I could hardly sleep. My stomach did flip-flops, and I tossed and turned until the sun came up.

I ate my breakfast on Sunday morning, well aware that it was customary to fast from confession until one received Holy Communion. "You gotta have a clean stomach to eat the body of Christ," Wanda had warned. "Maybe you better not eat breakfast."

"I'll eat all I want for breakfast," I had told her. Now, I could hardly chew my cereal or drink my milk.

I was grateful that no one in my family went to early Sunday Mass. My mother always told us she preferred to go on weekdays when there were few people and she could commune better with God. My older brothers never attended Mass, except for Easter Sunday and other high holy days. My aunt Maria went to afternoon Spanish Mass at one o'clock.

My mother gave me her blessing, as she did every Sunday, and sent me off to meet my friends. We were all going to attend ten o'clock Mass as usual.

I tried to act really calm when I saw everyone. I was surprised that even Joey was there. His folks didn't allow him to go inside our church. Joey was taking a chance disobeying them, so I knew he was there to see the action. There was no way I was gonna back out now.

"Are you really gonna do it?" asked Joey.

"Sure," I answered. "Why not!"

"You can still change your mind, you know."

"It's all right if she's chicken," said Casilda with a big phony smile. "It don't matter to me none."

"Look, girl," I snapped back, "I'm going through with it. So it don't matter what you want. I even had me a big breakfast—bacon and eggs." I lied. "And they tasted great. So, be cool . . . fool!"

When we arrived at church, we went right up to the front pew, because everyone except Joey was receiving Communion. I sat still during Mass, not daring to turn around. If anybody saw me, I sure didn't want to see them. Then the time came for Communion. Slowly but surely Casilda turned and stared into my eyes. As she walked up to the altar, she was followed by Wanda, Mary, and Ritchie. At first, I sat there feeling too numb to move. Maybe my friends wouldn't notice and I could stay put. But I knew I had no choice, so I stood and followed behind Ritchie.

I watched carefully and copied whatever Ritchie did. I knelt down at the altar and put my palms together and closed my eyes, as if in deep prayer. But I made sure to peek out of my right eye so I could see the priest. He was getting closer and closer. Then it was my turn, and the priest stood before me and made the sign of the cross. I stuck out my tongue and tasted the wafer, as thin and sticky as a postage stamp. I was amazed that it had no flavor at all. My heart was pounding so hard I couldn't move. But I took a deep breath and managed to open my eyes. Then I got to my feet and followed the others back to our pew.

As I sat down, I felt a sharp poke in my side. It was Casilda. "Now you'll go to hell for sure," she whispered.

"Stop chewing," Wanda warned me. "You're not supposed to chew the sacred body of Jesus, you know. Let it melt in your mouth!"

They both scared me half to death. I sat and silently prayed for mercy while I waited for something terrible to happen to me. But Mass continued and nothing unusual occurred.

Outside, the sun was shining and people stood

around talking to each other. I was glad that no one had stopped me or recognized me. Secretly, I thanked God for my good luck.

Joey was the first one to speak. "Wow!" he shrieked. "You did it, girl. I didn't think you would go through with it but—"

"Yeah!" interrupted Casilda. "But you committed a very big sin."

"For sure," agreed Mary. "And when you make your real Communion, you're gonna have to confess it."

"That's right." Wanda nodded. "And you're gonna have to do a lotta penance. Girl, I wouldn't want to be in your shoes for nothing!"

I felt pretty victorious now and ignored their warnings. After all, I had taken the dare and won.

"It don't bother me none," I smugly answered. "You see I ain't never going to confession. And I ain't never taking Communion again! Never!"

"Then you will just go to hell for absolute sure," said Casilda.

"Remember, my father says there ain't no hell!" I responded.

"But what does your mother think?" asked Casilda. "Tell us that!"

I couldn't answer with the truth, because I knew exactly what my mother thought. She would probably punish me worse than God. "I don't worry about that," I lied, then shrugged. "Anyway, I'm entitled to my own opinion, you know. This is a free country!" It was a favorite phrase from my older brother Gilbert.

As we walked along, the argument dwindled and we got to talking about other things. We spoke about school, and the end of the latest serial of the Green Hornet in the movie theaters, and the most recent Batman and Robin comic book.

Soon after, my mother took me to task and made sure I attended religious instruction. And about a year and a half later, I made my First Holy Communion. It was then that I finally owned up to most of my sins. These of course included lighting candles without contributing to the money box and receiving Communion without confession. I expected to be doing penance for at least a year. To my surprise, the priest mildly rebuked me and gave me a reasonable penance.

Afterward, I admitted to myself that it was a great relief to be able to confess and remove those dreaded sins from my conscience. But I never once admitted my relief to Casilda, Wanda, Mary, and little Ritchie, or even Jocy. After all was said and done, I had won the dare. My newfound clean conscience remained my secret.

Notes from

NICHOLASA MOHR

"From the moment my mother handed me some scrap paper, a pencil, and a few crayons, I discovered that by making pictures and writing letters I could create my own world . . . like 'magic.' In the small, crowded apartment I shared with my large family, making 'magic' permitted me all the space, freedom, and adventure that my imagination could handle. Drawing and painting were my first loves. Then, I began to write and to paint pictures with words.

When I was asked to write a story for this anthology, I decided to describe an event in my childhood that had tested my religious beliefs and my regard for authority figures. The incident I wrote about forced me to make some important decisions at an early age. Because my parents had such conflicting views about religion and spiritual beliefs, I had to find my own way. Upon reflection, I realized that my rebelliousness had a purpose. By taking my friends' dare, I was able to act independently, without taking either parent's side.

To this day, I continue to have a solid spiritual belief in a divine order very much like my mother's. I also strongly believe in many of the practical things my father taught me. Like him, I think that people must work hard and respect each other on this planet. Good deeds and faith in the capacity of our fellow human beings are necessary for our survival."

Reeve Lindbergh

FLYING

REEVE LINDBERGH

When I was your age, I was flying. I wasn't flying all the time, of course, and I didn't fly by myself, but there I was, nonetheless, on Saturday afternoons in the 1950s, several thousand feet in the air over the state of Connecticut, which is where I grew up. I sat in the back cockpit of a small airplane and looked down at the forests and the fields and the houses and the roads below me from an intense, vibrating height and hoped that my father, in the front cockpit, would not notice that I had cotton balls stuffed in my ears.

I always flew with my father, who had been a pioneer aviator in the 1920s and '30s. I think that he wanted to share his love for the air and for airplanes with his growing family, the way sports-minded fathers took their children to ball games on Saturdays and taught them to play catch afterward. My father took his children to the airport instead and taught them to fly.

Though he was the pilot on these flights, he did

not own the airplane. It was a sixty-five-horsepower Aeronca, with tandem cockpits, that he rented from a former bomber pilot whose name was Stanley. Stanley managed the airport, including the huge loaf-shaped hangar that served as a garage for repairs and maintenance to the aircraft, and he leased out the group of small planes tethered near the building like a fleet of fishing boats clustered around a pier.

It was Stanley, most often, who stood in front of the airplane and waited for my father to shout "Con-TACT!" from the cockpit window, at which time, Stanley gave the propeller a hefty downward shove that sent it spinning into action and started the plane shaking and shuddering on its way. The job of starting the propeller was simple but perilous. My father had warned us many times about the danger of standing anywhere near a propeller in action. We could list almost as well as he did the limbs that had been severed from the bodies of careless individuals "in a split second" by a propeller's whirling force. Therefore, each time that Stanley started the propeller, I would peer through its blinding whir to catch a glimpse of any pieces of him that might be flying through the air. Each time, I saw only Stanley, whole and smiling, waving us onto the asphalt runway with his cap in his hand and his hair blowing in the wind of our passing—"the propwash" my father called it.

My sister and my three brothers flew on Saturdays too. The older ones were taught to land and take off, to bank and dip, and even to turn the plane over in midair, although my second-oldest brother confessed that he hated this—it made him feel so dizzy. The youngest of my three brothers, only a few years older than me, remembers my father instructing him to "lean into the curve" as the plane made a steep sideways dive toward the ground. My brother was already off balance, leaning *away* from the curve, and hanging on for dear life. For my sister, our father demonstrated "weightlessness" by having the plane climb so steeply and then dive so sharply that for a moment she could feel her body straining upward against her seatbelt, trying to fight free, while our father shouted out from the front seat that one of his gloves was actually floating in midair.

"See the glove? See the glove?" He called to her over the engine noise and explained that if this state of weightlessness could continue, everything inside the plane would go up in the air. My sister nodded, not speaking, because, she told me later, everything in her stomach was going up in the air, too, and she did not dare open her mouth.

My oldest brother took to flying immediately and eventually got a pilot's license, though he ended up joining the navy and becoming a "frogman," spending as much time underwater with an aqualung and a wetsuit as he ever had spent in the air. What he secretly yearned to do during the flying years, though, was to jump right out of an airplane altogether, with a parachute. Finally, many years later, he had his chance and told me about it afterward. He stood at the open door of the airplane, with the parachute strapped to his back, wobbling back and forth at first, like a baby bird afraid to leave the nest. Then he jumped, fell about a hundred feet through the air, and only then pulled the cord that caused the chute to blossom around him like a great circular sail. Swaying under it, he floated toward the ground until he landed, fairly hard. I listened with astonishment; my brother's daring thrilled me to the bone.

My father on the other hand, along with most of the early aviators, was not impressed by the growing enthusiasm for parachute-jumping as a sport. Young daredevils like my brother could call it "sky-diving" if they wanted to, but the aviation pioneers referred to it disgustedly as "jumping out of a perfectly good airplane." In their day, a pilot only jumped when he had to: if it was absolutely certain that the airplane was headed for a crash and the parachute was his only hope for survival.

I was considered too young for aerial adventures when I flew, so I did not get dizzy or sick or worry about whether my parachute would open. It was only the noise that gave me trouble. I have never shared other people's enthusiasm for loudness. I don't like sudden sounds that make you jump with alarm, like the noises of fireworks or guns, or endless sounds that pound in your head so hard you can't think about anything else, like the commotion made by jackhammers and the engines of small airplanes. My sister felt exactly the same way. In fact, she was the one who showed me how to stuff cotton balls in my ears, secretly, for takeoff—when the engine noise was loudest—and for as long during the flight as we could get away with it.

Our father frowned upon the cotton balls. If he saw them, he would make us remove them. He claimed that they diminished the experience of flying and were in any case unnecessary: The engine noise was not so terribly loud that one couldn't get used to it; he certainly had done so. But my sister and I agreed that the only reason he and the other early aviators had "gotten used to" the noise of airplane engines close to their ears was that they had been deafened early on. We were not about to let this happen to us!

My mother, who had also flown back in the early days, always told us that she had loved her experience as a glider pilot best, because there was such extraordinary quiet all around her. In the absence of the usual aircraft engine noise, she could hear the songs of birds and sometimes even the trilling of insects, crickets or cicadas, on the grassy hillsides below. She said that because there was no noise, she could actually feel the power of air, the way it could push up under the wings of a glider and keep it afloat—like a boat on water—with the strength of unseen currents. She talked about "columns of air," stretching like massive tree trunks between earth and sky. "Just because you can't see the air doesn't mean there's nothing to it," she said. "Most of the really important things in our lives are invisible, anyway."

When it was my turn to fly with my father, I sat in the back cockpit and enjoyed the view all around me while he, in the front cockpit, flew the plane. I had a duplicate set of controls in back, with rudder pedals, a stick, and instruments, so that if I had been a true student pilot, I could have flown the plane myself, if called upon to do so. But since I was too young to understand or even to reach most of the controls in my cockpit, I just watched them move as if by magic, with no help from me at all, in response to my father's direction and will.

It looked easy. The stick in front of me, exactly like the one in front of my father in the forward cockpit, looked like the gearshift on our car. If it moved backward suddenly (toward me), it meant that my father had decided we were going up. There would be a rushing in my ears, in spite of the cotton, and as I looked over my father's head, through the front window of the aircraft, I would imagine that we were forcing our way right into heaven,

---

higher and higher through ever more brilliantly white banks of cloud. I sometimes daydreamed of bumping into angels, assembled on one of these cloud banks with their halos and their harps, or startling St. Peter at the pearly gates, or God himself in his sanctuary.

But then, as I watched, my stick would point forward again, toward what I could see, over the front pilot seat, of the back of my father's neck, with its trim fringe of gray hair and a khaki shirt collar. Then the airplane would nose down, giving a cockeyed view on all sides of blue sky and wooded hillsides and little tiny roads with buglike cars creeping along them, so very slowly. When we were flying, I was struck always by the insignificance of the world we had left behind. Nothing on the ground had speed, compared to us. Nothing looked real. Once I had climbed into the airplane, all of life seemed concentrated inside the loud space of it, shaking but steady, with my father's own hand on the controls. We were completely self-sufficient, completely safe, rock-solid in the center of the sky.

It was also a bit monotonous. My father did the same things and said the same things, loudly, over and over. I knew by heart that a pilot had to fly with a steady hand, with no sudden or jerky movements, just a little throttle here, a little wing dip there, always a light, even touch, always a calm approach. I knew all the stories about student pilots—those not already dismembered by propellers—who "froze" to the stick in a panic and could not let go, forcing the plane into a tragic nose-dive. There was no room in my father's lessons with me, his youngest and least experienced child, for soaring like the birds—no wind in the hair, no swooping and circling. We just droned along, my father and me.

And then, one Saturday afternoon, we didn't. I don't remember now exactly what made me understand there was something wrong with the airplane. I think there may have been a jerking sensation that repeated itself over and over. And I think too that there was a huge stillness in the air, a silence so enormous that it took me a moment to realize that it was actually the opposite of noise and not noise itself. The silence was there be-cause the engine had stalled. Perhaps the most pro-found moment of silence occurred when my father realized that it was not going to start again—no matter what he did. We were in the middle of the sky, on a sunny Saturday afternoon over Connecticut, in a plane without an engine.

I don't think there was any drop in altitude, not at first. What I noticed was my father's sudden alertness, as if he had opened a million eyes and ears in every di-rection. I heard him say something sharp on the air-planes's two-way radio to Stanley down below, and I could hear the crackle of Stanley's voice coming back. I knew enough not to say very much myself, although my father told friends later that I asked him once, in a conversational way, "Are we going to crash?" And when he told this part of the story, the part where I asked that question, he would laugh.

I don't remember being afraid of crashing. In fact, I don't remember fear at all, but I do remember excitement. At last something different was going to happen! I quickly took the cotton out of my ears because my father was talking. He told me that he was looking for a good place to land. We would have to land, he explained, because the engine wasn't working, and we could not land at the airport, because we were too far away to get there in time. (*In time for what?* I wondered.) He was looking for an open area to put the plane down in, right below us somewhere. We were now over a wooded hillside, dotted here and there with cow pastures: It would have to be a cow pasture. He spotted one that looked possible and circled down toward it.

There was nothing resembling a runway below us and no room to spare. He would have to tip the plane sideways and slip it into the pasture that way, somehow righting it and stopping its movement before it could hit any of the trees at the four edges of the field. We circled lower and lower, barely clearing the treetops, and then he told me to put my head down between my knees.

"Hold on!" my father said.

I didn't see the landing, because my head was down,

but I felt it: a tremendous series of bumps, as if we were bouncing on boulders, and then the plane shook and rattled to a stop. Then we took off our seatbelts and opened the doors and got out. I didn't see any cows in the pasture, but there were a bunch of people coming toward us from the road, and it looked as if one of them might be Stanley from the airport. I was careful to stay clear of the propeller.

Nobody could figure out how we had landed safely. They had to take the plane apart to get it out of the pasture, a week or more after that Saturday afternoon. But my father and I got a ride back to the airport with Stanley and drove home in plenty of time for dinner. We didn't talk much on the way home. My father seemed tired, though cheerful, and I was thinking.

I had found out something about him that afternoon, just by watching him work his way down through the air. I held on to the knowledge tightly afterward, and I still hold it to this day. I learned what flying was for my father and for the other early aviators, what happened to him and why he kept taking us up to try flying ourselves. As we came in through the trees, he was concentrating hard, getting the rudder and the flaps set, trying to put us in the best possible position for a forced landing, but he was doing more than that. He was persuading and coaxing and willing the plane to do what he wanted; he was leaning that airplane, like a bobsled, right down to where it could safely land. He could feel its every movement, just as if it were part of his own body. My father wasn't flying the airplane, he was *being* the airplane. That's how he did it. That's how he had always done it. Now I knew.

Notes from

REEVE LINDBERGH

"In the household where I grew up, writing was a kind of family habit, something the adults around me did every day without thinking too much about it, like taking a walk or brushing their teeth. I can't recall any time during my childhood when one of my parents was *not* engaged in writing a book. Most often, they were both busy writing books. This made us believe that the best thing you could do with an interesting idea or experience was to write it down. My sister Anne and I caught on to this notion early, and because of it, I think we both became writers before we grew up, though neither of us really believed we were writers until we had published books of our own, when we were parents ourselves.

I wrote this story about flying with my father because I remember it so clearly after all these years, but I've never told it, from my point of view, until now (though my father used to tell the story and others have too). When I became an adult, I found out how unusual it was to have had a 'forced landing' with Charles Lindbergh, this famous pioneer aviator I was related to, but at the time, it was just a little extra excitement during another Saturday afternoon of flying with my father. I wanted to write the experience down the way it really was, with the sense of excitement and the sense of normal everyday family life mixed up together. I think that's the way life really is."

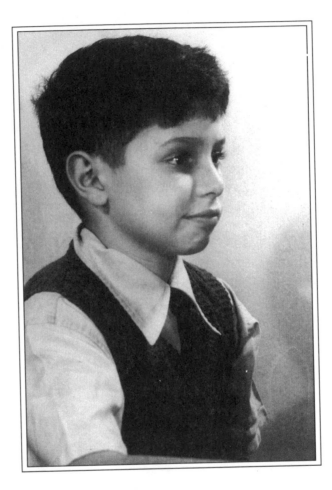

SCOUT'S HONOR

AVI

Back in 1946, when I was nine, I worried that I wasn't
tough enough. That's why I became a Boy Scout. Scouting, I thought, would make a man of me. It didn't take
long to reach Tenderfoot rank. You got that for joining.
To move up to Second Class, however, you had to meet
three requirements. Scout Spirit and Scout Participa-
tion had been cinchy. The third requirement, Scout
Craft, meant I had to go on an overnight hike in the
country. In other words, I had to leave Brooklyn, on my
own, for the first time in my life.

Since I grew up in Brooklyn in the 1940s, the only grass
I knew was in Ebbets Field where the Dodgers played.
Otherwise, my world was made of slate pavements,
streets of asphalt (or cobblestone), and skies full of tall
buildings. The only thing "country" was a puny pin oak
tree at our curb, which was noticed, mostly, by dogs.

I asked Scoutmaster Brenkman where I could find
some country. Now, whenever I saw Mr. Brenkman,

who was a church pastor, he was dressed either in church black or Scout khaki. When he wore black, he'd warn us against hellfire. When he wore khaki, he'd teach us how to build fires.

"Country," Scoutmaster Brenkman said in answer to my question, "is anywhere that has lots of trees and is not in the city. Many boys camp in the Palisades."

"Where's that?"

"Just north of the city. It's a park in Jersey."

"Isn't that a zillion miles from here?"

"Take the subway to the George Washington Bridge, then hike across."

I thought for a moment, then asked, "How do I prove I went?"

Mr. Brenkman looked deeply shocked. "You wouldn't *lie*, would you? What about Scout's honor?"

"Yes, sir," I replied meekly.

My two best friends were Philip Hossfender, whom we nicknamed Horse, and Richard Macht, called Max because we were not great spellers. They were also Scouts, Tenderfoots like me.

Horse was a skinny little kid about half my size whose way of arguing was to ball up his fist and say, "Are you saying . . . ?" in a threatening tone.

Max was on the pudgy side, but he could talk his way out of a locked room. More importantly, he always

Avi

seemed to have pocket money, which gave his talk real power.

I wasn't sure why, but being best friends meant we were rivals too. One of the reasons for my wanting to be tougher was a feeling that Horse was a lot tougher than I was, and that Max was a little tougher.

"I'm going camping in the Palisades next weekend," I casually informed them.

"How come?" Max challenged.

"Scout Craft," I replied.

"Oh, *that*," Horse said with a shrug.

"Look," I said, "I don't know about you, but I don't intend to be a Tenderfoot all my life. Anyway, doing stuff in the city is for sissies. Scouting is real camping. Besides, I like roughing it."

"You saying I don't?" Horse snapped.

"I'm not saying nothing," I said.

They considered my idea. Finally, Horse said, "Yeah, well, I was going to do that, but I didn't think you guys were ready for it."

"I've been ready for *years*," Max protested.

"Then we're going, right?" I said.

They looked around at me. "If you can do it, I can do it," Max said.

"Yeah," Horse said thoughtfully.

The way they agreed made me nervous. Now I really was going to have to be tough.

We informed our folks that we were going camping overnight (which was true) and that the Scoutmaster was going with us—which was a lie. We did remember what Mr. Brenkman said about honesty, but we were baseball fans too, and since we were prepared to follow Scout law—being loyal, helpful, friendly, courteous, kind, obedient, cheerful, thrifty, brave, clean, *and* reverent—we figured a 900 batting average was not bad.

So Saturday morning we met at the High Street subway station. I got there first. Stuffed in my dad's army surplus knapsack was a blanket, a pillow, and a paper bag with three white-bread peanut butter-and-jelly sandwiches—that is, lunch, supper, and Sunday breakfast. My pockets were full of stick matches. I had an old flashlight, and since I lived by the Scout motto—Be Prepared—I had brought along an umbrella. Finally, being a serious reader, I had the latest Marvel Family comics.

Horse arrived next, his arms barely managing to hold on to a mattress that seemed twice his size. As for food, he had four cans of beans jammed into his pockets.

Max came last. He was lugging a new knapsack that contained a cast-iron frying pan, a packet of hot dogs, and a box of saltine crackers—plus two bottles. One bottle was mustard, the other, celery soda. He also had a bag of Tootsie Rolls and a shiny hatchet. "To build a lean-to," he explained.

Max's prize possession, however, was an official Scout compass. "It's really swell," he told us. "You can't ever get lost with it. Got it at the Scout store."

"I hate that place," Horse informed us. "It's all new. Nothing real."

"This compass is real," Max retorted. "Points north all the time. You can get cheaper ones, but they point all different directions."

"What's so great about the north?" Horse said.

"That's always the way to go," Max insisted.

"Says who?" I demanded.

"Mr. Brenkman, dummy," Horse cried. "Anyway, there's always an arrow on maps pointing the way north."

"Cowboys live out west," I reminded them. They didn't care.

On the subway platform, we realized we did not know which station we were heading for. To find out, we studied the system map, which looked like a noodle factory hit by a bomb. The place we wanted to go (north) was at the top of the map, so I had to hoist Horse onto my shoulders for a closer look. Since he refused to let go of his mattress—or the tin cans in his pockets—it wasn't easy. I asked him—in a kindly fashion—to put the mattress down.

No sooner did he find the station—168th Street—than our train arrived. We rushed on, only to have

Horse scream, "My mattress!" He had left it on the platform. Just before the doors shut, he and I leaped off. Max, however, remained on the train. Helplessly, we watched as his horror-stricken face slid away from us. "Wait at the next station!" I bellowed. "Don't move!"

The next train took forever to come. Then it took even longer to get to the next stop. There was Max. All around him—like fake snow in a glass ball—were crumbs. He'd been so nervous he had eaten all his crackers.

"Didn't that make you thirsty?"

"I drank my soda."

I noticed streaks down his cheeks. Horse noticed them too. "You been crying?" he asked.

"Naw," Max said. "There was this water dripping from the tunnel roof. But, you said don't move, right? Well, I was just being obedient."

By the time we got on the next train—with all our possessions—we had been traveling for an hour. But we had managed to go only one stop.

During the ride, I got hungry. I pulled out one of my sandwiches. With the jelly soaked through the bread, it looked like a limp scab.

Horse, envious, complained *he* was getting hungry.

"Eat some of your canned beans," I suggested.

He got out one can without ripping his pocket too badly. Then his face took on a mournful look.

Avi

"What's the matter?" I asked.

"Forgot to bring a can opener."

Max said, "In the old days, people opened cans with their teeth."

"You saying my teeth aren't strong?"

"I'm just talking about history!"

"You saying I don't know history?"

Always kind, I plopped half my sandwich into Horse's hand. He squashed it into his mouth and was quiet for the next fifteen minutes. It proved something I'd always believed: The best way to stop arguments is to get people to eat peanut butter sandwiches. They can't talk.

Then we became so absorbed in our Marvel Family comics we missed our station. We got to it only by coming back the other way. When we reached street level, the sky was dark.

"I knew it," Max announced. "It's going to rain."

"Don't worry," Horse said. "New Jersey is a whole other state. It probably won't be raining there."

"I brought an umbrella," I said smugly, though I wanted it to sound helpful.

As we marched down 168th Street, heading for the George Washington Bridge, we looked like European war refugees. Every few paces, Horse cried, "Hold it!" and adjusted his arms around his mattress. Each time we paused, Max pulled out his compass, peered at it, then announced, "Heading north!"

I said, "The bridge goes from east to west."

"Maybe the bridge does," Max insisted with a show of his compass, "but guaranteed, *we* are going north."

About then, the heel of my left foot, encased in a heavy rubber boot over an earth-crushing Buster Brown shoe, started to get sore. Things weren't going as I had hoped. Cheerfully, I tried to ignore the pain.

The closer we drew to the bridge, the more immense it seemed. And the clouds had become so thick, you couldn't see the top or the far side.

Max eyed the bridge with deep suspicion. "I'm not so sure we should go," he said.

"Why?"

"Maybe it doesn't have another side."

We looked at him.

"No, seriously," Max explained, "they could have taken the Jersey side away, you know, for repairs."

"Cars are going across," I pointed out.

"They could be dropping off," he suggested.

"You would hear them splash," Horse argued.

"I'm going," I said. Trying to look brave, I started off on my own. My bravery didn't last long. The walkway was narrow. When I looked down, I saw only fog. I could feel the bridge tremble and sway. It wasn't long before I was convinced the bridge was about to collapse. Then a ray of hope struck me: Maybe the other guys had chickened out. If they had, I could quit because of *them*. I glanced back. My heart sank. They were coming.

After they caught up, Horse looked me in the eye and said, "If this bridge falls, I'm going to kill you."

A quarter of a mile farther across, I gazed around. We were completely fogged in.

"I think we're lost," I announced.

"What do we do?" Horse whispered. His voice was jagged with panic. That made me feel better.

"Don't worry," Max said. "I've got my compass." He pulled it out. "North is that way," he said, pointing in the direction we had been going.

Horse said, "You sure?"

"A Scout compass never lies," Max insisted.

"*We* lied," I reminded him.

"Yeah, but this is an *official* Scout compass," Max returned loyally.

"Come on," Max said and marched forward. Horse and I followed. In moments, we crossed a metal bar on the walkway. On one side, a sign proclaimed: NEW YORK; on the other, it said: NEW JERSEY.

"Holy smoke," Horse said with reverence as he straddled the bar. "Talk about being tough. We're in two states at the same time."

It began to rain. Max said, "Maybe it'll keep us clean."

"You saying I'm not clean?" Horse shot back.

Ever friendly, I put up my umbrella.

We went on—Max on one side, Horse on the other, me in the middle—trying to avoid the growing puddles. After a while, Max said, "Would you move the umbrella? Rain is coming down my neck."

"We're supposed to be roughing it," I said.

"Being in the middle isn't roughing it," Horse reminded me.

I folded the umbrella up so we all could get soaked equally.

"Hey!" I cried. "Look!" Staring up ahead, I could make out tollbooths and the dim outlines of buildings.

"Last one off the bridge is a rotten egg!" Horse shouted and began to run. The next second, he tripped and took off like an F-36 fighter plane. Unfortunately, he landed like a Hell-cat dive-bomber as his mattress unspooled before him and then slammed into a big puddle.

Max and I ran to help. Horse was damp. His mattress was soaked. When he tried to roll it up, water cascaded like Niagara Falls.

"Better leave it," Max said.

"It's what I sleep on at home," Horse said as he slung the soaking, dripping mass over his shoulder.

When we got off the bridge, we were in a small plaza. To the left was the roadway, full of roaring cars. In front of us, aside from the highway, there was nothing but buildings. Only to the right were there trees.

"North is that way," Max said, pointing toward the trees. We set off.

"How come you're limping?" Horse asked me. My foot *was* killing me. All I said, though, was, "How come you keep rubbing your arm?"

"I'm keeping the blood moving."

We approached the grove of trees. "Wow," Horse exclaimed. "Country." But as we drew closer, what we found were discarded cans, bottles, and newspapers—plus an old mattress spring.

"Hey," Max cried, sounding relieved, "this is just like Brooklyn."

I said, "Let's find a decent place, make camp, and eat."

It was hard to find a campsite that didn't have junk. The growing dark didn't help. We had to settle for the place that had the least amount of garbage.

Max said, "If we build a lean-to, it'll keep us out of the rain." He and Horse went a short distance with the hatchet.

Seeing a tree they wanted, Max whacked at it. The hatchet bounced right out of his hand. There was not even a dent in the tree. Horse retrieved the hatchet and checked the blade. "Dull," he said.

"Think I'm going to carry something sharp and cut myself?" Max protested. They contented themselves with picking up branches.

I went in search of firewood, but everything was wet. When I finally gathered some twigs and tried to light them, the only thing that burned was my fingers.

Meanwhile, Horse and Max used their branches to build a lean-to directly over me. After many collapses—which didn't help my work—they finally got the branches to stand in a shaky sort of way.

"Uh-oh," Horse said. "We forgot to bring something for a cover."

Max eyed me. "Didn't you say you brought a blanket?"

"No way!" I cried.

"All in favor of using the blanket!"

Horse and Max both cried, "Aye."

Only after I built up a mound of partially burned match sticks and lit *them,* did I get the fire going. It proved that where there's smoke there doesn't have to be much fire. The guys meanwhile draped my blanket over their branch construction. It collapsed twice.

About an hour after our arrival, the three of us were gathered inside the tiny space. There was a small fire, but more light came from my flickering flashlight.

"No more rain," Horse said with pride.

"Just smoke," I said, rubbing my stinging eyes.

"We need a vent hole," Horse pointed out.

"I could cut it with the hatchet," Max said.

"It's my mother's favorite blanket."

"And you took it?" Max said.

I nodded.

"You *are* tough," Horse said.

Besides having too much smoke in our eyes and being wet, tired, and in pain, we were starving. I almost said something about giving up, but as far as I could see, the other guys were still tough.

Max put his frying pan atop my smoldering smoke. After dumping in the entire contents of his mustard bottle, he threw in the franks. Meanwhile, I bolted down my last sandwich.

"What am I going to eat?" Horse suddenly said.

"Your beans," I reminded him.

Max offered up his hatchet. "Here. Just chop off the top end of the can."

"Oh, right," Horse said. He selected a can, set it in front of him, levered himself onto his knees, then swung down—hard. There was an explosion. For a stunned moment, we just sat there, hands, face, and clothing dripping with beans.

Suddenly Max shouted, "Food fight! Food fight!" and began to paw the stuff off and fling it around.

Having a food fight in a cafeteria is one thing. Having one in the middle of a soaking wet lean-to with cold beans during a dark, wet New Jersey night is another. In seconds, the lean-to was down, the fire kicked over, and Max's frankfurters dumped on the ground.

"The food!" Max screamed, and began to snatch up

the franks. Coated with mustard, dirt, grass, and leaves, they looked positively prehistoric. Still, we wiped the franks clean on our pants then ate them—the franks, that is. Afterward, we picked beans off each other's clothes—the way monkeys help friends get rid of lice.

For dessert, Max shared some Tootsie Rolls. After Horse swallowed his sixteenth piece, he announced, "I don't feel so good."

The thought of his getting sick was too much. "Let's go home," I said, ashamed to look at the others. To my surprise—and relief—nobody objected.

Wet and cold, our way lit by my fast-fading flashlight, we gathered our belongings—most of them, anyway. As we made our way back over the bridge, gusts of wind-blown rain pummeled us until I felt like a used-up punching bag. By the time we got to the subway station, my legs were melting fast. The other guys looked bad too. Other riders moved away from us. One of them murmured, "Juvenile delinquents." To cheer us up, I got out my comic books, but they had congealed into a lump of red, white, and blue pulp.

With the subways running slow, it took hours to get home. When we emerged from the High Street Station, it was close to midnight.

Before we split up to go to our own homes, we just stood there on a street corner, embarrassed, trying to figure out how to end the day gracefully. I was the one who said, "Okay, I admit it. I'm not as tough as you guys. I gave up first."

Max shook his head. "Naw. I wanted to quit, but I wasn't tough enough to do it." He looked to Horse.

Horse made a fist. "You saying I'm the one who's tough?" he demanded. "I hate roughing it!"

"Me too," I said quickly.

"Same for me," Max said.

Horse said, "Only thing is, we just have to promise not to tell Mr. Brenkman."

Grinning with relief, we simultaneously clasped hands. "No matter what," Max reminded us.

To which I added, "Scout's Honor."

Notes from
AVI

"I am a twin and that meant—and still means—sharing with my twin sister Emily. For example, usually it's me who tells the jokes while she laughs. Or, if we're at a party together, Emily does most of the talking, while I tend to be the listener.

When we were kids, one of her jobs was remembering. Thus, though we were in the same class from nursery school through seventh grade, Emily remembers our classmates' and teachers' names. I recall just my friends' names. In short, my memories of childhood are only of those things I did without her.

So, when asked to write a story about when I was young, I recalled the time I was trying to be a Boy Scout, my first attempt at an overnight camping trip. Emily wasn't there.

Keep in mind that 'Scout's Honor' is a piece of fiction. Though I can't recall the actual words we spoke, much less the moment to moment events, the broad outlines of that fiasco are true. What's more, I recall that, even then, we thought it was all pretty funny.

At the age when this story takes place—

though I was a voracious reader—it had never occurred to me that I might become a writer. But I *was* an inventor of stories, which I—and my friends—acted out, much as described in my book *Who Was that Masked Man, Anyway?* Only during high school, when I was told I was a bad writer, did I decide to prove that I could write. As for my twin sister, she too is a writer. She writes poetry and nonfiction. So you see, we still divide things up."

Francesca Lia Block

BLUE

FRANCESCA LIA BLOCK

La's mother wasn't there, waiting in front of the school in the dusty white Volvo station wagon. La sat on the lawn and watched all the other mothers gathering their children. When the sun started to go down, she walked home along the broad streets lined with small houses, thick, white, leaflike magnolia blossoms crisping brown at the edges, deadly pink oleander, eucalyptus trees grayed with car exhaust. The air smelled of gasoline, chlorine, and fast food meat, with an occasional whiff of mock orange too faint to disguise much with its sweetness.

La walked up the brick path under the birch tree that shivered in the last rays of sun and went into the pale-blue wood frame house. She found her father sitting in the dark.

"Daddy?" she whispered.

He looked up, and his swollen, unshaven face made her step backward as if she had been hit.

"What's wrong?" La asked. "Where's Mom?" She wanted to say Mommy, but she didn't want to use baby words.

"Your mother left." He sounded as though there were wet tissues in his throat.

"Where's Mommy?" she asked again.

"How many times do I have to tell you?" He never raised his voice to her. "She left us. She's gone."

"Where did she go?"

"I don't know."

La took a step toward her father, but the look in his eyes made her back away into her bedroom and shut the door. She sat on her bed and stared at the wall she had helped her mother paint with wildflowers, pale and heathery; now they seemed poisonous. La looked at Emily, H.D., Sylvia, Ann, Christina, and Elizabeth sitting on the love seat. Her mother had named them after her favorite poets. They stared back with blank doll eyes.

La wanted to cry, but she couldn't. She felt like a Tiny Tears doll with no water inside.

"La," said a voice.

She jumped and turned around. The closet door was open a crack. La never left the closet door open. She was afraid that demons would come out and get her in the night.

"La," the voice whispered.

She held her breath.

Francesca Lia Block

The closet door opened a little more, and a tiny shadow tiptoed out.

Maybe, she thought later, Blue was really just her tears. Maybe Blue was the tears that didn't come.

The creature came into the light. It had thin, pale, slightly bluish skin. It blinked at La with blue eyes under glittery eyelashes.

"Who are you?" La felt a slice of fear. "Why are you here?"

"For you."

La rubbed her eyes. "Are you a demon?"

The creature looked about to cry. La shook her head, trying to make it go away.

"Now you should sleep, I think," and the creature reached out its tiny blue fingers with the bitten nails and touched La's forehead.

Almost immediately La was asleep.

She dreamed about the creature holding her mother's hand and running through a field of wildflowers.

"Blue," La's mother said in the dream. "Your name is Blue."

The house where La lived looked completely different now. When La's mother was living there, the garden had been wild, but a garden—now the flowers were burnt up; crabgrass stitched the dirt. There had been bread baking, bowls of fruit, Joni Mitchell singing on the stereo, light coming through the windows. Now, the only light in the living room was from the television's glow. La's father stopped writing the novel he had been working on. Every night after he got home from the college, he corrected papers and watched TV. La's mother had been a student in his English class, and he had fallen in love with her when he read her poetry. Wanting to protect her from a world that seemed too harsh, he had not understood how she dreamed of living in a commune, dancing barefoot in parks, and reading her poems, wearing silver Indian bells and gypsy shawls, even though these were the things that had drawn him to her.

La remembered when she was a little girl, how her mother had held her close and said, "Can you see the little dolls in Mommy's eyes?" La had seen two tiny Las there. As she got older, she still looked for herself inside her mother. Now she tried to find that La in her father, but his eyes were closed to her, dull and blind.

La fixed herself a bowl of cornflakes and went into her room to talk to Blue.

"Did you know my mother?" La asked

"I can tell you things about her."

"How do you know?" La was suspicious.

"I know because I know you."

"Like what?"

"She wrote poetry."

La thought about the journals with the stiff, creamy

paper and thick, bumpy black covers that her mother hid at the bottom of the closet. La had looked for them after her mother had left, but they were gone. She had tried to remember some of the poems her mother had read to her from the books. She had opened a tiny bottle of French perfume that was sitting on her mother's marble-top dressing table. As she put a drop to her throat, she remembered something about a girl dancing in a garden while a black swan watched her with hating eyes and one poem about a woman with black roses tattooed on her body. Something about a blue child calling to a frightened woman from out of the mists—begging.

"Did she want me?" La asked Blue.

"At first she was scared of you. You were so red and noisy, and you needed so much."

La could feel her eyes stinging, but Blue said, "Then she changed her mind. After a while, you were all she really cared about."

"Then why did she leave?"

Blue went and perched on the window sill. "That I don't know."

One day at lunch, Chelsea Fox came and sat next to La. Chelsea had shiny lemonade-colored hair tied up high in a ponytail, and she was wearing pink lip gloss that smelled like bubble gum. La thought she was the most beautiful girl she had ever seen. She made you want to give her things.

"Don't you have any friends?" Chelsea demanded.

La shrugged.

"Why not?"

La said, "I like to play by myself."

"I used to be that way," Chelsea said. "I started talking when I was real little, and the other kids didn't understand what I was saying. They just sat in the sandbox and stared at me. So I made up an imaginary friend I talked to. But my mother told me it wasn't healthy."

"I do have one friend." La had been wanting to talk about Blue so much. And now Chelsea Fox was asking! La's heart started to pound against her. She felt as if she were made of something thin and breakable, with this one heavy thing inside of her. "Blue is blue and lives in my closet."

Chelsea laughed, all tiny teeth like mean pearls. "You still have an imaginary friend?"

"Blue is real."

Chelsea made a face at La, flipped her hair, picked up her pink metal Barbie lunch box, and walked away. La crushed her brown paper bag with her fist on the lunch table where she sat alone now. Milk from the small carton inside the bag seeped onto the peeling, scratched table and dripped down.

After that, no one talked to La at all. Chelsea Fox had

a birthday party. La saw the invitations with the ballerinas on them. She waited and waited. But she was the only girl who didn't get one.

When Miss Rose found out, she asked La and Chelsea to stay after school. Miss Rose was a very thin, freckled, red-haired woman who always wore shades of green or pink.

"Chelsea, don't you think you should invite La to your birthday party?" Miss Rose said.

La looked down to hide her red face. She remembered what Blue had told her about how red she had been as a baby, how it had frightened her mother.

Chelsea shrugged.

"Go ahead, Chelsea, ask La. It isn't nice to leave her out."

Chelsea smiled so her small white teeth showed. They reminded La of a doll's. "La, would you like to come to my party?"

La was afraid to look up or move. She hated Miss Rose then.

"She doesn't want to," Chelsea said.

"I think she does," said Miss Rose. "Don't you, La?"

"Okay," La whispered, wanting her teacher to shut up.

"Why don't you bring an invitation in tomorrow?" Miss Rose said.

"Just don't bring any imaginary friends," Chelsea hissed when they were dismissed onto the burning asphalt. La imagined Chelsea spitting her teeth out like weapons. The air smelled grimy and hot like the pink rubber handballs.

La walked past some boys playing volleyball. The insides of her wrists were chafed from trying to serve at recess; her knees were scraped from falling down in softball; her knuckles raw from jacks. Sometimes her knees and knuckles were embedded with bits of gravel, speckled with blood. She had mosquito bites on her back.

"There goes Wacko," one of the boys shouted.

La felt chafed, scraped, raw, and bitten inside too.

La wasn't planning to go to Chelsea Fox's birthday party, but she saved the invitation anyway. La's father saw it. He hardly spoke to his daughter anymore, but that morning, he said, "Is that a party invitation?"

La nodded.

"Good," said her father. "It's about time you did something like that."

La went mostly because her father had seemed interested in her again and she wanted to please him—she wanted him to see her. But the next weekend, when he drove her to Chelsea's tall house with the bright lawn, camellia-and-rose-filled garden, the balloons tied to the mailbox, and the powder-blue Mercedes in the driveway, he was as far away as ever.

Maybe it is better that he doesn't offer to walk me in, she thought. *I don't want them to see him anyway.*

She wanted to go home and play with Blue, but instead, she jumped out of the car and went up to the door where a group of girls waited with their mothers.

Chelsea answered, wearing a pastel jeans outfit. The girls kissed her cheek and gave her presents. When it was La's turn, she gulped and brushed her lips against Chelsea's face. Chelsea reached up to her cheek and rubbed away the kiss with the back of her hand.

Inside, the house was decorated in floral fabrics—huge peonies and chrysanthemums—and lit up with what seemed like hundreds of lamps. Little pastel girls were running around screaming. There was one room all made of glass and filled with plants and leafy, white iron furniture. In the middle was a long table heaped with presents. La sat in a corner of the room by herself. After a while, Chelsea's mother came in, leading a chorus of "Happy Birthday" and holding a huge cake covered in wet-looking pink-frosting roses. Chelsea's mother had a face like a model on a magazine cover—cat eyes, high cheekbones, and full pouting lips. She was tall and slender, her blonde hair piled on top of her head, with little wisps brushing down against her long pearled neck. La watched Chelsea blow out eleven candles in one breath.

"I'll get my wish!"

She probably did get her wish, La thought, watching Chelsea's small hands tearing open the presents—Barbies, Barbie clothes, Barbie cars, stuffed toys, roller skates, jeans, T-shirts, a glittery magenta bike with a white lattice basket covered with pink plastic flowers.

La had brought the almost-empty bottle of perfume that had belonged to her mother. Even though the fragrance inside it was the only thing that seemed to bring La's mother back, La had decided to give it to Chelsea. Maybe it would make Chelsea like her, La thought. It was her greatest treasure.

When Chelsea opened it, she said, "What's this? It's been used!" and threw it aside.

Chelsea's mother let the girls stay up until midnight, and then she told them to get their sleeping bags. La's belonged to her father—blue with red flannel ducks on the inside. The other girls had pastel sleeping bags with Snoopy or Barbie on them. La put her bag down in a corner and listened to the sugar-wild giggles all around her.

Suddenly, she heard Chelsea say, "La, tell us about your imaginary friend. La has an imaginary friend."

"She gave you an imaginary present," Amanda Warner said.

Snickers. They sounded mean with too much cake. La was silent.

"Come on." The girls squealed. "Tell us."

La said, "No I don't."

"Your mom left because you are so weird," said Katie Dell.

"I think her mom was pretty weird too. She was a hippy," said Chelsea.

La buried down in the musty red flannel of her sleeping bag.

Blue, she thought, to keep herself from crying.

Near morning, when the other girls were finally quiet, warm thin arms the color of Chelsea Fox's eyes wrapped around La's waist.

"Write about it," Blue whispered. "Write it all."

That was the same thing Miss Rose said the next day in class. "I want us all to write about someone we love." She looked straight at La. La noticed for the first time how sad Miss Rose's brown eyes were.

La went home and shut the door of her room. She lay down on her belly on the floor, with a pen and a piece of paper. There was a creaking sound, and the closet door opened. Blue came out.

"What are you doing?"

"I'm supposed to write about someone I love. I want to write about my mom, but I'm afraid."

Blue began to whisper things in La's ear. She picked up her pen and wrote.

La wrote how she had been named La for the musical

sound and also for the city they lived in—not for the dry, flat, chain-link-fenced, train-track-lined, used-car-lot-full valley where their house was, but for the city over the hill. In that city, La's mother—wearing a paisley dress, her long hair hanging to her waist—took La to eat honey-colored cornbread at a restaurant with a mural of an Indian temple on the outdoor courtyard wall and soft candle cubes flickering like chants on every table. She took La to the museum where they saw jewelry in the shapes of fairies with stained-glass wings; to a temple in the hills full of gentle-faced Buddha statues and people planting trees, the air almost lavender with clouds of incense. They walked around the lake tucked into the Hollywood hills, feeling the cool, wet air on their cheeks, looking out at the expanse of water and the small, magical bridge lined with white globes; La imagined a princess receiving her guests there. They rode wooden horses on the carousel at the pier, feeling the smooth, wooden horse flanks, caressing the ridges of wooden roses on the saddles, watching the circle of lights that seemed to make the tinkling music. On dusty trails, they rode real horses, and La's mother pointed out the wildflowers peeking at them from behind rocks. When they got home, they zigzagged handfuls of wildflower seeds into the earth—primrose, columbine, lupine, and cornflower. They painted wildflowers on the walls of La's room—"So you will always have them," her mother said.

La wrote about her mother coming into her room at night sometimes, to read La poetry by Emily and H.D. in the pinkish light, the words like her mother's perfume wafting around them. Sometimes, La's mother read her own poems. La felt the secret of sadness bonding them together then.

"I will love you forever," La's mother had said. "No matter where I am on the planet, I am always loving you."

La wrote about all of that and about the perfume bottle shaped like a teardrop that had brought her mother back.

"This is wonderful, La," Miss Rose said. "Would you like to read it to the class?"

La shook her head, cringing, pressing her back against hard wood and metal.

"I really think you should," said Miss Rose.

Chelsea Fox said, "I'd love to hear your story." She said it so sweetly that for a moment La believed her. But then she saw Chelsea glance over at Amanda Warner, and a silent laugh swelled the air between them.

"Go ahead," Miss Rose said.

La couldn't breathe. She felt like throwing up.

But when she started to read, something happened. She forgot about Chelsea Fox, Amanda Warner, and everyone else in the class. The words La and Blue had written cast their spell—even over La. She could smell the perfume and bittersweet wildflowers; she could hear Joni Mitchell's *For the Roses* playing softly.

When La was finished, she looked up. Everyone was silent, watching her.

"That was beautiful," Miss Rose finally said.

The bell rang, and everyone scattered. La went into the fluorescent-lit, brown and beigy-pink hallway. Her heart was beating fast but in a different way this time. She felt as if she had physically touched everyone in the room, as if she had played her favorite song for Miss Rose and lifted an open, tear-shaped bottle of fragrance to Chelsea Fox's face.

"Your mom sounds like she was cool," Chelsea said, catching up with La. "My mom isn't like that. She doesn't spend time with me except to go shopping and stuff." La looked into Chelsea's blue eyes. The pupils were big and dark. There was no laughter in them now. La nodded.

Chelsea tossed her hair and ran to catch up with her friends.

When La got home, she ran inside to tell Blue. Her father wasn't on the couch watching TV where La expected him. She heard his typewriter keys and peeked into his office. The windows were open and Vivaldi was playing; he had a cup of coffee at his fingertips.

"Daddy," La said.

When she handed him the story, his eyes changed.

"It's about Mom," La said, but she knew he knew.

"I'm writing something about her too," he said. He held out his hand, and she went to him. He sat up and kissed her forehead.

"Thank you, honey." He looked as though he hadn't slept or eaten for days. But he took off his glasses then, and La saw two small images of herself swimming in the tears in his eyes.

La went to her room to tell Blue. In the closet, there were only clothes and shoes and shadows now.

Notes from
FRANCESCA LIA BLOCK

"I wrote 'Blue' based on certain aspects of my childhood, although much of it is very far from my reality. I lived in a house like the one described in the story, and I had an active imagination that I used in my writing as a way to feel connected to others. The main difference between my life and the story is that my parents were always together and very supportive of me.

It was their love and encouragement that influenced my decision to become a writer. I was at first hesitant to present the parents in 'Blue' in a negative light, since the story was meant to be at least semi-autobiographical, but I made certain choices because I wanted to add drama to the piece. My father, who is no longer living, always told me to write whatever I needed to write and not to be afraid or inhibited as an artist."

AUTHOR BIOGRAPHIES

MARY POPE OSBORNE is the author of many highly acclaimed novels for young readers as well as picture books, middle-grade biographies, and collections of myths and fairy tales. Her most recent works include the Magic Tree House series, *American Tall Tales,* the Spider Kane mystery series, and the young-adult novel *Haunted Waters.* She was recently elected president of the Authors Guild, the leading organization for writers in the United States. She lives in New York City.

LAURENCE YEP grew up in San Francisco and now lives on the California coast. He is the award-winning author of a number of books for children and young adults, including *Dragonwings* and *Dragon's Gate,* both Newbery Honor Books; *The Star Fisher,* winner of the Christopher Medal; and *Child of the Owl,* which won the Boston Globe–Horn Book Award. He has also worked as a playwright and has adapted his own *Dragonwings* for the theater.

JAMES HOWE has written many books for children and young adults, including the Sebastian Barth mystery series, *Morgan's Zoo, A Night Without Stars,* and *The New Nick Kramer, or My Life as a Babysitter.* He is best known for his Bunnicula series about a vampire rabbit, which has received a number of state and readers' choice awards, including Vermont's Dorothy Canfield Fisher Children's Book Award for *Bunnicula: A Rabbit-Tale of Mystery.* He currently lives in Hastings-on-Hudson, New York.

KATHERINE PATERSON left China just before the U.S. entered World War II. Since then she has lived all over the United States and in Japan. For nearly ten years she has lived in Vermont and hopes never to move again. She has written books set both in China (*Rebels of the Heavenly Kingdom*) and Japan (including National Book Award winner, *The Master Puppeteer*). She has won two Newbery Awards for *Bridge to Terabithia* and *Jacob Have I Loved*. *The Great Gilly Hopkins* is a Newbery Honor Book and a National Book Award winner. *Lyddie*, her "Vermont novel," was on the IBBY Honors List.

WALTER DEAN MYERS is from Harlem, New York, and now lives in New Jersey. He is the author of many acclaimed books for children and young adults, including *Brown Angels* and *Scorpions*, a Newbery Honor Book. He has won the Coretta Scott King Award four times for his books *The Young Landlords*, *Motown and Didi*, *Fallen Angels*, and *Now Is Your Time!: The African-American Struggle for Freedom*.

SUSAN COOPER is a novelist, screenwriter, and playwright. Of her many books, the best-known are the five fantasy novels in the young-adult sequence, The Dark Is Rising, which have won awards around the world, including a Newbery Medal and a Newbery Honor Medal. She has also written screenplays for television, including the Hallmark/CBS productions of *Foxfire* and *To Dance with the White Dog*. In collaboration with Hume Cronyn, she wrote the original play with songs *Foxfire*, which ran on Broadway, and a screen adaptation of *The Doilmaker*, starring Jane Fonda, which received the Humanitas Prize, a Christopher Award, and an Emmy nomination. Susan Cooper currently lives in Cambridge, Massachusetts.

NICHOLASA MOHR has written a number of books for young people, including *Nilda*; *El Bronx Remembered*, winner of the American Book Award and a National Book Award finalist; *Felita*; and *Growing Up Inside the Sanctuary of My Imagination*, a memoir. She was born in *El Barrio*, grew up in the Bronx, and now makes her home in Brooklyn. From 1994 through 1995, she was writer-in-residence at Richmond College, the American International University in London, England.

REEVE LINDBERGH, the daughter of aviator Charles Lindbergh and author Anne Morrow Lindbergh, has written many picture books and adult novels. Her works for children include *The Day the Goose Got Loose, Johnny Appleseed, What Is the Sun?, View from the Air: Charles Lindbergh's Earth and Sky,* and *Benjamin's Barn* and *The Midnight Farm,* both winners of the Redbook Children's Picturebook Award. She currently lives in northern Vermont.

AVI currently lives in Providence, Rhode Island. He is the author of several highly acclaimed novels, including *Nothing But the Truth* and *The True Confessions of Charlotte Doyle,* both of which were Newbery Honor Books and Boston Globe–Horn Book Award winners. He has also written *The Fighting Ground,* which received the Scott O'Dell Award for best historical fiction. A former librarian, he has taught children's literature and writing and is an active member of the Authors' Guild.

FRANCESCA LIA BLOCK is best known for her young-adult novels in the Weetzie Bat series: *Weetzie Bat, Witch Baby, Cherokee Bat and the Goat Guys,* and *Missing Angel Juan,* most of which are ALA Best Books for Young Adults and *School Library Journal* Best Books. All of these have also been named ALA Recommended Books for Reluctant Young Adult Readers. She has also written *The Hanged Man* and another Weetzie story, *Baby Be-Bop,* as well as two adult fantasy novels. Francesca Lia Block lives in Los Angeles, California, the setting of the majority of her young-adult novels.

Amy Ehrlich, the editor of *When I Was Your Age*, notes that "writing begins with observation. The authors in this collection, like all children, felt things deeply. But they also were able to observe their feelings and therefore to remember them as well. Those memories are a writer's most durable tool." Amy Ehrlich has been an editor and a writing teacher and is the author of more than twenty-five books for young readers.